CREATIVE
CASSEROLE
COOKERY

GOOD HOUSEKEEPING
STEP-BY-STEP COOKERY

CREATIVE CASSEROLE COOKERY

Guild Publishing/Ebury Press
LONDON

This edition published 1985 by
Book Club Associates
By arrangement with Ebury Press

Consultant editor: Jeni Wright
Editor: Miren Lopategui
Design by Mike Leaman
Drawings by Bill le Fever and John Woodcock
Photographs by Laurie Evans
Cover photograph by Paul Kemp

Cover photograph: Boeuf Bourguignon (page 14)

Filmset by Advanced Filmsetters (Glasgow) Ltd

Printed and bound in Italy by
New Interlitho, S.p.a., Milan

CONTENTS

COOKERY NOTES

Follow either metric or imperial measures for the recipes in this book as they are not inter-changeable. Sets of spoon measures are available in both metric and imperial size to give accurate measurement of small quantities. All spoon measures are level unless otherwise stated. When measuring milk we have used the exact conversion of 568 ml (1 pint).

* Size 4 eggs should be used except when otherwise stated.

† Granulated sugar is used un-less otherwise stated.

OVEN TEMPERATURE CHART

°C	°F	Gas mark
110	225	$\frac{1}{4}$
130	250	$\frac{1}{2}$
140	275	1
150	300	2
170	325	3
180	350	4
190	375	5
200	400	6
220	425	7
230	450	8
240	475	9

KEY TO SYMBOLS

$\boxed{1.00}$* Indicates minimum preparation and cooking times in hours and minutes. They do not include prepared items in the list of ingredients; calcu-lated times apply only to the method. An asterisk * indicates extra time should be allowed, so check the note below symbols.

⌂ Chef's hats indicate degree of difficulty of a recipe: no hat means it is straightforward; one hat slightly more complicated; two hats indicates that it is for more advanced cooks.

£ Indicates a recipe which is good value for money; £ £ indicates an expensive recipe. No £ sign indicates an inexpensive recipe.

✳ Indicates that a recipe will freeze. If there is no symbol, the recipe is unsuitable for freezing. An asterisk * indicates special freezer instructions so check the note immediately below the symbols.

$\boxed{309 \text{ cals}}$ Indicates calories per serving, including any sugges-tions (e.g. cream, to serve) given in the ingredients.

METRIC CONVERSION SCALE

LIQUID			SOLID		
Imperial	Exact conversion	Recommended ml	Imperial	Exact conversion	Recommended g
$\frac{1}{4}$ pint	142 ml	150 ml	1 oz	28.35 g	25 g
$\frac{1}{2}$ pint	284 ml	300 ml	2 oz	56.7 g	50 g
1 pint	568 ml	600 ml	4 oz	113.4 g	100 g
$1\frac{1}{2}$ pints	851 ml	900 ml	8 oz	226.8 g	225 g
$1\frac{3}{4}$ pints	992 ml	1 litre	12 oz	340.2 g	350 g

For quantities of $1\frac{3}{4}$ pints and over, litres and fractions of a litre have been used.

14 oz	397.0 g	400 g
16 oz (1 lb)	453.6 g	450 g

1 kilogram (kg) equals 2.2 lb.

CREATIVE CASSEROLE COOKERY

Don't dismiss casseroles as just warming winter food for the family. The recipes in this book will soon convince you that casseroles make exciting eating at any time of year, on virtually any occasion.

In the first five chapters of the book you will find casserole recipes for all the different kinds of meat—Beef and Veal, Lamb, Pork and Bacon, Variety Meats and Sausages, Poultry and Game. Here there is a wide-ranging selection of traditional and everyday recipes alongside exotic dishes from all over the world. Chapters on Fish and Shellfish and Vegetables follow, which give a new dimension to casserole cookery and offer inspiring ideas for alternative main courses. All the recipes in these chapters are photographed in colour, and there are helpful step-by-step illustrations within the methods, which make the recipes clear and easy to follow.

In the back section of the book, called Useful Information and Basic Recipes, there are chapters on equipment for casserole making, preparation of ingredients and different cooking techniques, plus instructions on freezing and re-heating. Recipes for vegetable accompaniments are also here, plus fruit casseroles for desserts and basic recipes for stocks, sauces, toppings, marinades and flavourings.

Beef and Veal

In this chapter you will find a wide variety of beef and veal recipes, from everyday family casseroles to special occasion dishes for entertaining. Long, slow cooking is the perfect method for the less tender cuts of beef and veal, and you will find that once the casserole is in the oven you can quite literally walk away and leave it to look after itself.

BEEF, WALNUT AND ORANGE CASSEROLE

| 2.45 | £ | 679 cals |

Serves 4

900 g (2 lb) chuck steak, cut into 2.5 cm (1 inch) cubes

40 g (1½ oz) seasoned plain flour

45 ml (3 tbsp) vegetable oil

1 onion, skinned and chopped

4 celery stalks, trimmed and roughly chopped

150 ml (¼ pint) unsweetened orange juice

600 ml (1 pint) beef stock

bouquet garni

2 garlic cloves, skinned and crushed

2 oranges

100 g (4 oz) broken walnuts

salt and freshly ground pepper

orange shreds, to garnish

1 Toss the meat in the seasoned flour. Heat the oil in a flame-proof casserole and fry the onion and celery for about 5 minutes. Add the meat and fry for 5 minutes until browned. Add the orange juice, stock, bouquet garni and garlic.

2 Bring to the boil, cover and cook in the oven at 170°C (325°F) mark 3 for 2 hours.

3 Meanwhile, peel the oranges over a plate, removing all the pith. Cut the flesh into segments.

4 Add the walnuts and orange segments to the casserole, together with any juice that may have collected on the plate. Continue to cook for a further 30 minutes until the meat is tender. Taste and adjust the seasoning. Serve the casserole garnished with orange shreds.

Menu Suggestion
This special occasion casserole is best served with new potatoes, or jacket baked potatoes topped with soured cream and snipped chives.

BEEF, WALNUT AND ORANGE CASSEROLE

Chuck steak is recommended for this dinner party casserole; although one of the more expensive cuts of beef for casseroling, it is worth buying in this case for its lean, tender flesh. From the shoulder of the animal, chuck steak is one of the best-quality cuts of braising or stew-ing beef you can buy—some butchers sell it in thick slices, others sell it ready cut up into cubes, as required for this recipe. Other cuts of stewing beef can be substituted such as cubed flank, blade, skirt and even shin, but they will be fattier and coarser, and so need longer cooking.

MARINATED SPICED BEEF

2.15* ✳* 340 cals

* plus 3 days marinating and at least 8 hours cooling and refrigeration before serving; freeze in marinade before cooking

Serves 6

450 ml (¾ pint) red wine
150 ml (¼ pint) red wine vinegar
1 onion, skinned and sliced
10 ml (2 tsp) ground allspice
50 g (2 oz) soft brown sugar
1.1 kg (2½ lb) rolled topside of beef
15 ml (1 tbsp) whole cloves
salt and freshly ground pepper
30 ml (2 tbsp) vegetable oil
mustard and horseradish sauce, to serve

1 Make the marinade. In a large bowl, mix together the wine, vinegar, onion, allspice and sugar.

2 Stud the beef with the cloves. Sprinkle all over with salt and pepper, then place the joint in the marinade.

3 Cover the bowl with cling film and marinate in the refrigerator for 3 days, turning it each day.

4 When ready to cook the beef, remove it from the marinade and pat dry with absorbent kitchen paper.

5 Heat the oil in a large flame-proof casserole, add the beef and brown quickly on all sides over high heat. Pour in the marinade, bring slowly to boiling point, then lower the heat, cover and simmer for 2 hours or until the beef is tender.

6 Remove the casserole from the heat and leave to cool. Refrigerate for at least 8 hours, turning the beef occasionally during this time.

7 To serve. Remove the meat from the liquid and slice neatly. Serve cold, with mustard and horseradish sauce.

Menu Suggestion

Serve this sliced cold beef as part of a buffet party spread or summer luncheon with a selection of salads—potato and beetroot salads would go especially well.

MARINATED SPICED BEEF

Try not to skimp on the marinating time in this recipe. Three days may seem rather a long time, but you will find it helps enormously to tenderise topside, which can sometimes be a rather dry, tough joint of meat.

The acid in the wine and the wine vinegar in the marinade helps break down the connective tissue in the topside, and the longer the beef is left, the more tender it will be after cooking.

SUSSEX STEW

| 3.00 | £ | ✳ | 533 cals |

Serves 4

30 ml (2 tbsp) plain flour

5 ml (1 tsp) dried thyme

salt and freshly ground pepper

900 g (2 lb) stewing steak, in one piece

30 ml (2 tbsp) beef dripping or lard

1 large onion, skinned and sliced

300 ml ($\frac{1}{2}$ pint) sweet stout

30 ml (2 tbsp) mushroom ketchup

thyme sprigs, to garnish

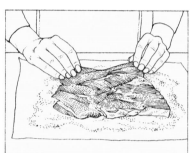

1 Mix the flour with the thyme and salt and pepper and spread out on a large flat plate or sheet of greaseproof paper. Coat the meat in the flour.

2 Melt the dripping or lard in a flameproof casserole. Add the onion slices and fry gently for 5 minutes until soft but not coloured. Remove with a slotted spoon and set aside. Add the beef to the casserole, increase the heat and fry quickly until browned on both sides.

3 Return the onion slices to the casserole, then pour in the stout mixed with the mushroom ketchup. Bring slowly to boiling point, then cover with a lid and cook in the oven at 150°C (300°F) mark 2 for 2–2½ hours until tender. Taste and adjust seasoning. Serve the casserole garnished with thyme sprigs.

Menu Suggestion

Sussex Stew has plenty of thick, rich gravy. Accompanied by creamed potatoes and carrots tossed in chopped fresh herbs, it makes a perfectly balanced family meal.

SUSSEX STEW

Sussex Stew is an old, traditional English dish, in which stewing beef is slowly braised in sweet stout and mushroom ketchup until wonderfully succulent and full of flavour. Although an everyday family dish, take care with your choice of ingredients for best results. Sweet stout rather than ordinary stout or ale is essential for the richness of the gravy, and mushroom ketchup gives it a special tang, which helps offset the sweetness of the stout. Mushroom ketchup is easy to find in large supermarkets and delicatessens; sold in bottles, it keeps indefinitely, so is well worth buying as it can be used in other dishes.

BOEUF BOURGUIGNON (BEEF IN WINE)

| 2.30 | £ £ ✳ | 585 cals |

Serves 4

50 g (2 oz) butter

30 ml (2 tbsp) vegetable oil

100 g (4 oz) bacon in a piece, rinded and diced

900 g (2 lb) braising steak or topside, cubed

1 garlic clove, skinned and crushed

45 ml (3 tbsp) plain flour

salt and freshly ground pepper

bouquet garni

150 ml ($\frac{1}{4}$ pint) beef stock

300 ml ($\frac{1}{2}$ pint) red Burgundy

12 small onions, skinned

175 g (6 oz) button mushrooms

chopped fresh parsley, to garnish

1 Heat half the butter and oil in a flameproof casserole and fry the bacon for 5 minutes. Drain.

2 Reheat the fat and fry the meat in small amounts for about 8 minutes until browned.

3 Return the bacon to the casserole with the garlic. Sprinkle the flour over and stir in.

4 Add seasoning, the bouquet garni, stock and wine, then bring to the boil, stirring. Cover and cook in the oven at 170°C (325°F) mark 3 for 1½ hours.

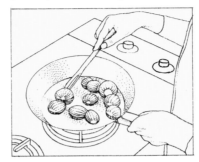

5 Meanwhile, heat the remaining butter and oil together and sauté the whole onions for about 10 minutes until glazed and golden brown. Remove from the pan. Add the mushrooms to the pan and fry for 5 minutes.

6 Add the mushrooms and onions to the casserole and cook for a further 30 minutes until the meat is tender.

7 Remove the bouquet garni. Skim off the surface fat. Serve garnished with chopped parsley.

Menu Suggestion
Serve this classic French dish for a dinner party with new potatoes tossed in melted butter and chopped fresh parsley, followed by a green salad tossed in vinaigrette dressing.

CARBONNADE DE BOEUF *(BEEF IN BEER)*

| 4.15 | £ | ✳ | 781 cals |

Serves 4

salt and freshly ground pepper

900 g (2 lb) stewing steak, cut into 5 cm (2 inch) cubes

50 g (2 oz) beef dripping or butter

75 g (3 oz) lean bacon, rinded and chopped

60 ml (4 tbsp) plain flour

300 ml (½ pint) beer, plus a little extra, if necessary

300 ml (½ pint) beef stock

30–45 ml (2–3 tbsp) vinegar

10 ml (2 tsp) soft brown sugar

pinch of grated nutmeg

450 g (1 lb) onions, skinned and chopped

1 garlic clove, skinned and chopped

bouquet garni

four 1 cm (½ inch) slices of French bread

15 ml (1 tbsp) French mustard

chopped fresh parsley, to garnish

1 Season the meat. Heat the fat in a frying pan and fry the meat for about 5 minutes until browned. Add the bacon and fry for 3 minutes. Remove the meat and bacon from the pan.

2 Stir the flour into the pan and brown lightly. Gradually add the beer, stock, vinegar, sugar and nutmeg, stirring continuously until the mixture thickens.

3 Layer meat, bacon, onions and garlic in a casserole. Pour the sauce over and add bouquet garni.

4 Cover and cook in the oven at 150°C (300°F) mark 2 for 3½–4 hours until the meat is tender. Add a little more beer while cooking, if necessary.

5 Thirty minutes before serving, remove the bouquet garni and skim off the fat. Spread the French bread with the mustard and place on top of the stew, pushing the slices into the liquid. Return uncovered to the oven for 30 minutes until well browned. Garnish with chopped parsley.

Menu Suggestion

Suitable for an informal supper party, Carbonnade de Boeuf tastes good with buttered ribbon noodles or boiled rice, and needs no further accompaniment other than a simple green salad.

CARBONNADE DE BOEUF

This is a version of a very old recipe—one of the great classics of French provincial cookery, which was originally Flemish and cooked in locally brewed Belgian beer. There are many versions of carbonnade to be found all over northern France and Belgium nowadays, and they all differ slightly, but without exception they always include beer and onions. The beer should be the lager or light ale type if the dish is to taste anything like the original Flemish version.

DAUBE DE BOEUF (BRAISED BEEF WITH OLIVES)

`3.15*` ✳* `564 cals`

* plus 4–6 hours marinating; freeze in marinade before cooking

Serves 6

1.1 kg (2½ lb) rolled top rump of beef

50 g (2 oz) stuffed green olives, sliced

salt and freshly ground pepper

300 ml (½ pint) red wine

30 ml (2 tbsp) olive oil

30 ml (2 tbsp) beef dripping or lard

75 ml (3 fl oz) brandy

1 large onion, skinned and sliced

3 carrots, peeled and sliced

4 tomatoes, skinned and roughly chopped

6 rashers of smoked streaky bacon, rinded

2 garlic cloves, skinned and halved

bouquet garni

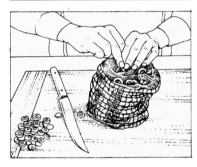

1 Make several deep incisions in the joint of beef and insert the slices of olive.

2 Put the beef in a bowl and sprinkle with salt and pepper. Mix together the wine and olive oil and pour over the beef. Cover the bowl and leave to marinate for 4–6 hours.

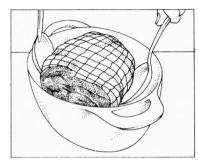

3 Remove the beef from the marinade and pat dry with absorbent kitchen paper. Reserve the marinade. Melt the dripping or lard in a large flameproof casserole, add the beef and brown quickly on all sides over high heat.

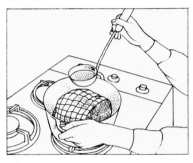

4 Heat the brandy gently in a separate small pan or a ladle. Turn off the heat under the casserole, pour in the brandy and set it alight. When the flames have died down, remove the beef from the casserole and set it aside.

5 Add the onion and carrots to the casserole and fry gently for 5 minutes until onion is soft but not coloured. Add the tomatoes and stir well to mix, then remove the vegetables with a slotted spoon.

6 Put the bacon rashers in the bottom of the casserole, then cover with the vegetables. Bury the garlic and bouquet garni in the vegetables, then place the beef on top and pour over the reserved marinade mixed with enough water to come halfway up the meat. Add salt and pepper to taste and bring slowly to boiling point.

7 Cover the casserole with foil or greaseproof paper, then the lid. Cook in the oven at 150°C (300°F) mark 2 for 2½ hours or until the beef is tender.

8 Blot the surface of the sauce with absorbent kitchen paper to remove as much fat as possible and remove the bouquet garni. Taste and adjust the seasoning of the sauce before serving.

Menu Suggestion

An informal main course, Daube de Boeuf is traditionally served in France with boiled potatoes or noodles and a tossed green salad.

DAUBE DE BOEUF

Almost every region of France has its own version of Daube de Boeuf. The word *daube* comes from *daubière*, which is the French word for a covered casserole. This recipe is for a joint of beef, which the French sometimes lard with strips of fat to make more moist. Bite-sized pieces of chuck steak can be used instead of one large piece of meat, whichever you prefer.

BLADE BEEF WITH BRANDY

| 2.45 | ✳* | 340 cals |

* freeze after step 5

Serves 6

6 thick slices of blade of beef, each weighing 150 g (5 oz)

30 ml (2 tbsp) vegetable oil

25 g (1 oz) butter or margarine

175 g (6 oz) onions, skinned and thickly sliced

225 g (8 oz) carrots, peeled and thickly sliced

45 ml (3 tbsp) brandy

150 ml ($\frac{1}{4}$ pint) beef stock

1 garlic clove, skinned and crushed

salt and freshly ground pepper

175 g (6 oz) button mushrooms, sliced

chopped fresh parsley, to garnish (optional)

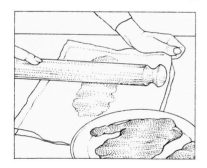

1 Trim any fat or skin off the meat and bat out the pieces of meat between sheets of grease-proof paper.

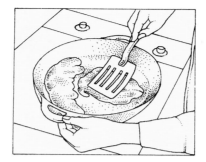

2 Heat the oil and fat in a medium flameproof casserole and fry the pieces of meat, one or two at a time, pressing the meat on to the hot surface of the pan with a fish slice until browned. Remove from the casserole.

3 Add the onions and carrots and fry for 5 minutes until lightly browned. Replace the meat.

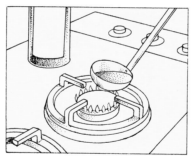

4 Heat the brandy in a ladle, ignite and pour over the meat. When the flames have subsided, add the stock, garlic and seasoning to the casserole.

5 Bring to the boil, cover and cook in the oven at 170°C (325°F) mark 3 for $1\frac{1}{2}$–$1\frac{3}{4}$ hours or until the meat is almost tender.

6 Strain the juices, then return to the meat with the sliced mushrooms. Cover the casserole and continue to cook for a further 15 minutes.

7 Lift the meat out of the cooking liquor and arrange in a warmed shallow serving dish.

8 Bring the liquor to the boil and reduce slightly by cooking for 1–2 minutes, stirring continuously. Adjust the seasoning.

9 To serve. Spoon the juices over the meat. Garnish with chopped fresh parsley.

Menu Suggestion
An excellent main course dish for an informal dinner party. Serve with creamed or jacket baked potatoes and a seasonal green vegetable such as broccoli.

BLADE BEEF WITH BRANDY
Blade of beef is an excellent cut for long, slow cooking in the oven. From the shoulder of the cow, it is sold with the blade bone removed, usually cut into thick slices rather than cubed as other stewing meats. Blade is always fairly lean, but don't worry if you notice a thick seam or two of fat running through it—this will break down during the long, slow cooking and give the finished meat a moist, tender quality.

BEEF STEW WITH HERBY DUMPLINGS

3.00 £ ❄* 519 cals

* freeze stew without dumplings

Serves 6

25 g (1 oz) lard

900 g (2 lb) stewing steak, cut into 2.5 cm (1 inch) cubes

350 g (12 oz) carrots, peeled and sliced

350 g (12 oz) turnips, peeled and cut into chunks

350 g (12 oz) onions, skinned and sliced

25 g (1 oz) plain flour

750 ml (1¼ pints) beef stock

salt and freshly ground pepper

bouquet garni

100 g (4 oz) self-raising flour, sifted

50 g (2 oz) shredded suet

15 ml (1 tbsp) chopped fresh mixed herbs or 5 ml (1 tsp) dried

1 Melt the lard in a frying pan and fry the meat for about 8 minutes until browned. Remove the meat to a large casserole.

2 Fry the carrots, turnips and onions in the remaining fat in the pan for about 5 minutes until the onions are softened. Add the vegetables to the meat.

3 Sprinkle the plain flour into the pan, stir well to mix with the fat, then gradually stir in the stock. Bring to the boil, stirring, then season well and pour over the meat and vegetables. Add the bouquet garni.

4 Cover and cook in the oven at 170°C (325°F) mark 3 for about 2–2¼ hours until the meat is almost tender.

5 To make the dumplings. Mix the self-raising flour, suet, herbs and a pinch of salt together. Bind with sufficient cold water to give an elastic dough. Divide into 12 pieces and roll into balls.

6 When the meat is almost tender, discard the bouquet garni and add the dumplings. Cover the casserole again, and cook for a further 20 minutes until the dumplings are risen.

Menu Suggestion

A substantial dish, this stew needs only a seasonal vegetable to accompany it.

KOFTA CURRY

| 1.30 | 🍴 | 375 cals |

Serves 4

450 g (1 lb) lean minced beef
5 ml (1 tsp) garam masala
5 ml (1 tsp) ground cumin
15 ml (1 tbsp) finely chopped fresh
   coriander
salt and freshly ground pepper
30 ml (2 tbsp) ghee or vegetable oil
3 onions, skinned and chopped
1 garlic clove, skinned and chopped
2.5 cm (1 inch) piece fresh root
   ginger, peeled and chopped
1 green chilli, seeded and chopped
3 green cardamoms
4 whole cloves
6 black peppercorns
5 cm (2 inch) cinnamon stick
1 bay leaf
10 ml (2 tsp) ground coriander
2.5 ml ($\frac{1}{2}$ tsp) ground turmeric
300 ml ($\frac{1}{2}$ pint) natural yogurt
150 ml ($\frac{1}{4}$ pint) water
fresh coriander, to garnish
   (optional)

1 Mix together the beef, garam masala, cumin, fresh coriander, salt and pepper. Set aside.

2 Make the sauce. Heat the ghee or oil in a large saucepan and fry the onions, garlic, ginger and chilli for 10 minutes until golden.

3 Add the cardamoms, cloves, peppercorns, cinnamon and bay leaf and fry over a high heat for 3 minutes. Add the ground coriander, turmeric and salt to taste. Fry for 3 minutes.

4 Gradually add the yogurt, a tablespoon at a time, stirring thoroughly after each addition, then the water. Simmer for 10 minutes or until thickening.

5 Meanwhile, shape the meat mixture into 16 small balls. Lower the meatballs into the sauce so that they are completely covered. Cover and simmer gently for 30 minutes or until cooked.

6 To serve. Skim off any excess fat, then transfer to a warmed serving dish and garnish with chopped coriander.

Menu Suggestion

These Indian-style meatballs are traditionally accompanied by boiled or pilau rice and a mixed vegetable curry. Mango chutney, lime pickle and sliced banana can also be served.

CHILLI CON CARNE (SPICED BEEF AND BEANS)

| 2.45* | £ | ✳ | 409 cals |

* plus overnight soaking of dried beans

Serves 6

225 g (8 oz) dried red kidney beans, soaked overnight

30 ml (2 tbsp) vegetable oil

2 onions, skinned and chopped

900 g (2 lb) chuck steak, cubed

1 large garlic clove, skinned and crushed

1 bay leaf

1 green chilli, seeded and chopped

5 cm (2 inch) stick cinnamon

4 whole cloves

1.25 ml ($\frac{1}{4}$ tsp) dried oregano

1.25 ml ($\frac{1}{4}$ tsp) dried marjoram

2.5 ml ($\frac{1}{2}$ tsp) cayenne pepper

1.25 ml ($\frac{1}{4}$ tsp) sesame seeds

15 ml (1 tbsp) salt

freshly ground pepper

30–45 ml (2–3 tbsp) chilli seasoning or 2.5 ml ($\frac{1}{2}$ tsp) chilli powder

30 ml (2 tbsp) tomato purée

793 g (28 oz) can tomatoes

pinch of sugar

5 ml (1 tsp) malt vinegar

2 coriander sprigs

1 Drain the soaked beans and place in a saucepan of cold water. Bring to the boil and boil rapidly for 10 minutes, then drain.

2 Meanwhile, heat the oil in a flameproof casserole and fry the onions for 5 minutes until softened. Add the meat and cook for about 8 minutes until browned.

3 Add the next twelve ingredients to the meat and continue to fry for 2 minutes, stirring constantly. Add the tomato purée, tomatoes with their juice, sugar, vinegar, coriander and the boiled and drained beans.

4 Bring to the boil, cover and cook in the oven at 170°C (325°F) mark 3 for about 2$\frac{1}{4}$ hours until the meat is tender.

Menu Suggestion
Chilli con Carne is traditionally eaten with plain boiled rice. If you find it hot, serve it with natural yogurt and sliced cucumber to cool the palate.

CHILLI CON CARNE

If you forget to soak the red kidney beans overnight for this dish, there is still no reason why it shouldn't be made on the day. One short-cut method is to make the casserole without the beans altogether, then 10 minutes before serving, simply stir in a can of ready-cooked red kidney beans (drained and rinsed) and heat through. Another alternative is the hot-soak method for dried beans: put the beans in a pan, cover with cold water and bring to the boil. Boil for 10 minutes, then turn off the heat, cover the pan and leave to soak for 1 hour. Continue from step 1 of the recipe.

VEAL IN TOMATO AND WINE SAUCE

| 2.30 | £ £ ✳ | 414 cals |

Serves 4

25 g (1 oz) butter

30 ml (2 tbsp) olive oil

3 onions, skinned and chopped

2 carrots, peeled and chopped

1–2 celery stalks, trimmed and chopped

1 garlic clove, skinned and crushed

4 pieces shin of veal, 900 g (2 lb) total weight

plain flour, for coating

salt and freshly ground pepper

300 ml ($\frac{1}{2}$ pint) dry white wine

350 g (12 oz) tomatoes, skinned and chopped, or 396 g (14 oz) can tomatoes

150 ml ($\frac{1}{4}$ pint) chicken stock

2 strips of lemon peel

1 bay leaf

15 ml (1 tbsp) chopped fresh parsley

2.5 ml ($\frac{1}{2}$ tsp) dried basil

1.25 ml ($\frac{1}{4}$ tsp) dried thyme

1 Melt the butter with the oil in a large frying pan. Add the chopped vegetables and the garlic and fry gently for 5 minutes until lightly coloured.

2 With a slotted spoon, transfer the vegetables to a large flame-proof casserole which will hold the pieces of veal in one layer.

3 Coat the pieces of veal in flour seasoned with salt and pepper. Add to the frying pan and fry over moderate heat until browned on all sides.

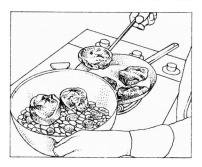

4 Place the pieces of browned veal on top of the vegetables in the casserole.

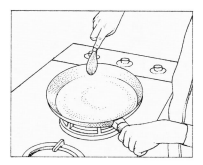

5 Pour the wine into the frying pan and bring to boiling point. Stir constantly with a wooden spoon, scraping base and sides of pan to dislodge any sediment.

6 Add the remaining ingredients and simmer, stirring, until the tomatoes are broken down. Add seasoning to taste, then pour over the veal in the casserole.

7 Cover and cook in the oven at 180°C (350°F) mark 4 for about 2 hours or until the veal is tender. Taste and adjust seasoning before serving.

Menu Suggestion
Serve with Italian risotto for a dinner party main course with a difference. A chilled dry Italian white wine such as Orvieto, Frascati or Soave would be an ideal drink.

GOULASH
(BEEF STEW WITH PAPRIKA)

| 3.10 | ✳ | 354 cals |

Serves 8

1.4 kg (3 lb) stewing veal or braising steak

75 g (3 oz) butter or margarine

700 g (1½ lb) onions, skinned and thinly sliced

450 g (1 lb) carrots, peeled and thinly sliced

45–60 ml (3–4 tbsp) paprika

30 ml (2 tbsp) plain flour

900 ml (1½ pints) chicken stock

60 ml (4 tbsp) dry white wine

salt and freshly ground pepper

142 ml (5 fl oz) soured cream

1 Cut the meat into 4 cm (1½ inch) pieces. Melt the fat in a frying pan and fry the meat, a little at a time, until browned. Drain and place in a shallow oven-proof dish.

2 Fry the onions and carrots in the fat remaining in the pan for about 5 minutes until lightly browned. Add the paprika and flour and fry for 2 minutes. Gradually stir in the stock, wine and seasoning. Bring to the boil and pour over the meat.

3 Cover tightly and cook in the oven at 150°C (300°F) mark 2 for 2¾ hours until tender. When cooked, pour the soured cream over the goulash and serve.

Menu Suggestion
Goulash is traditionally served with dumplings or noodles. An unusual alternative to these accompaniments is a dish of boiled new potatoes and sautéed button mushrooms, tossed together with chopped fresh herbs and some melted butter.

GOULASH

This recipe for goulash is simple and straightforward — typical of the kind of goulash to be found in Austria. Hearty and warming, it is the ideal dish to serve in cold weather, especially in the depths of winter when snow is on the ground — the Austrians frequently eat goulash or bowls of goulash soup to keep them warm at lunchtime after a morning's skiing. Goulash is also very popular in Hungary, where it is often made with extra ingredients such as red and green peppers, mushrooms and tomatoes, resulting in a more flamboyant-looking dish with a stronger flavour. When buying paprika to make goulash, look for the variety in the silver sachet from Hungary which is labelled *süss* (sweet).

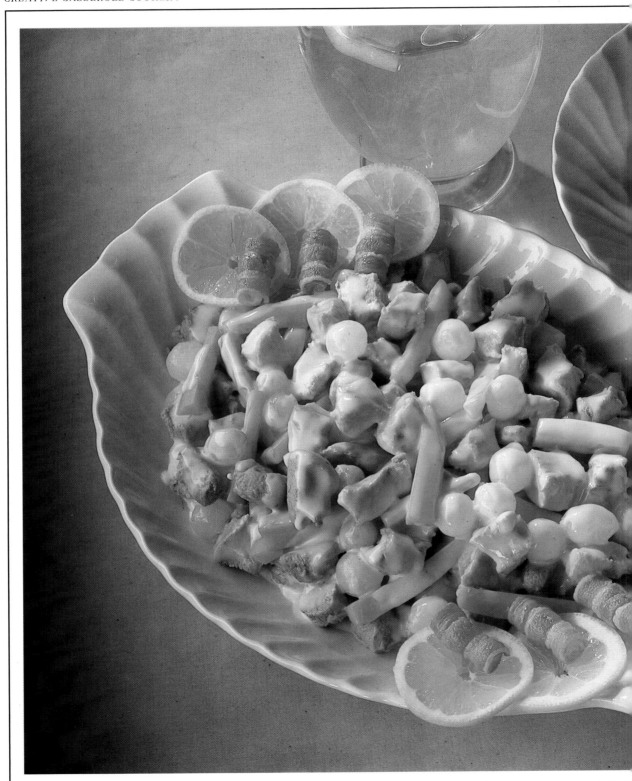

VEAL IN CREAM SAUCE

| 1.45 | 🥄 | 469 cals |

Serves 6

900 g (2 lb) stewing veal or braising steak, cubed

450 g (1 lb) carrots, peeled and cut into fingers

225 g (8 oz) button onions, skinned

bouquet garni

150 ml ($\frac{1}{4}$ pint) white wine

900 ml ($1\frac{1}{2}$ pints) water

salt and freshly ground pepper

chicken stock, if necessary

50 g (2 oz) butter

50 g (2 oz) plain flour

300 ml ($\frac{1}{2}$ pint) single cream

lemon slices and grilled bacon rolls, to garnish

1 Cover the meat with cold water, bring to the boil and boil for 1 minute. Strain in a colander and rinse under cold running water to remove all scum. Place the meat in a flameproof casserole.

2 Add the carrots and onions to the casserole with the bouquet garni, wine, water and plenty of seasoning. Bring slowly to the boil, cover and simmer gently for about $1\frac{1}{4}$ hours or until the meat is tender.

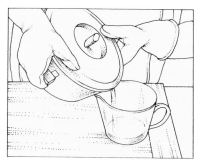

3 Strain off the cooking liquor, make up to 750 ml ($1\frac{1}{4}$ pints) with stock if necessary, reserve. Keep the meat and vegetables warm in a covered serving dish.

4 Melt the butter in a saucepan and stir in the flour, cook gently for 1 minute. Remove from the heat and stir in the strained cooking liquor; season well. Bring to the boil, stirring all the time, and cook gently for 5 minutes.

5 Take the sauce off the heat and stir in the cream. Warm very gently, without boiling, until the sauce thickens slightly. Adjust the seasoning. Pour the sauce over the meat. Garnish with lemon slices and bacon rolls.

Menu Suggestion
Veal in Cream Sauce is a very rich dinner party dish. Serve with plain boiled rice and a green salad tossed in a vinaigrette dressing.

PAUPIETTES DE VEAU
(STUFFED VEAL ROLLS)

| 1.30 | 🍲 | £ £ ✳* | 438 cals |

* freeze after step 6

Serves 6

50 g (2 oz) butter

1 small onion, skinned and finely chopped

1 celery stalk, trimmed and finely chopped

5 ml (1 tsp) paprika

175 g (6 oz) button mushrooms, finely chopped

150 g (5 oz) granary or wholemeal breadcrumbs

finely grated rind of ½ lemon

30 ml (2 tbsp) chopped fresh parsley

1 egg size 6, beaten

salt and freshly ground pepper

6 veal escalopes or thin slices of rump steak, each weighing about 175 g (6 oz)

plain flour, for coating

30 ml (2 tbsp) vegetable oil

300 ml (½ pint) chicken stock

150 ml (¼ pint) dry cider or white wine

bouquet garni

90 ml (6 tbsp) single cream

extra paprika, for sprinkling

1 Make the stuffing. Melt 25 g (1 oz) butter in a large flame-proof casserole, add the onion, celery and paprika and fry gently for 5 minutes until soft. Add the mushrooms and fry for a few minutes more until the juices run.

2 Transfer the vegetables to a bowl and add the bread-crumbs, lemon juice and the parsley. Stir well to mix, then bind with the beaten egg and add seasoning to taste.

3 Put the veal or beef between two sheets of greaseproof paper and bat out thinly with a meat mallet or rolling pin. Cut each piece in half.

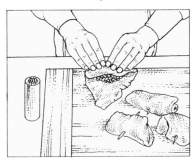

4 Place the pieces of meat in a single layer on a floured board and divide stuffing between them.

5 Roll the meat up around the stuffing and secure with wooden cocktail sticks. Coat in seasoned flour.

6 Heat the remaining butter with the oil in the casserole, add the meat rolls and try in two batches over moderate heat until browned on all sides. Drain on absorbent kitchen paper. Pour in the stock and cider or wine and bring slowly to boiling point, stir-ring constantly to scrape the sediment from base of casserole. Lower the heat and add the bouquet garni, then cover and simmer for 30–40 minutes until the meat is tender.

Menu Suggestion

A special dinner party dish, best served with a fresh green vegetable such as courgettes, French beans or mange-touts.

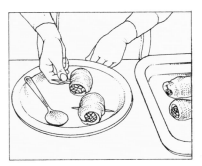

7 Remove the meat rolls from the casserole with a slotted spoon and place on a plate. Re-move the cocktail sticks; keep meat hot on a warmed serving platter.

8 Remove the bouquet garni and stir in the cream. Heat through without boiling, then adjust seasoning. Pour over the rolls, sprinkle lightly with paprika and serve immediately.

VEAL CHOPS IN WINE

| 1.10 | £ £ ✳* | 453 cals |

* freeze after step 3

Serves 4

30 ml (2 tbsp) plain flour

salt and freshly ground pepper

4 thick veal or pork loin chops

25 g (1 oz) butter

15 ml (1 tbsp) olive oil

150 ml ($\frac{1}{4}$ pint) dry white wine

juice of $\frac{1}{2}$ lemon

10 ml (2 tsp) chopped fresh
    tarragon or 5 ml (1 tsp) dried

60 ml (4 tbsp) port

60 ml (4 tbsp) double cream

chopped fresh tarragon, to garnish

1 Place the flour in a bowl, and season with salt and pepper. Dip the chops in the seasoned flour, ensuring that both sides are evenly coated.

2 Melt the butter with the oil in a shallow flameproof dish which will hold chops in a single layer. Fry chops over moderate heat until browned on all sides.

3 Pour in the wine and lemon juice and bring slowly to boiling point. Add the tarragon and cover with a lid or foil. Cook in the oven at 170°C (325°F) mark 3 for 45 minutes until tender.

4 With a spatula, transfer the chops to a warmed serving platter. Keep warm in the oven turned to its lowest setting.

5 Put the baking dish on top of the cooker and stir in the port. Bring to the boil, stirring constantly with a wooden spoon and scraping the base and sides of the dish to dislodge any sediment.

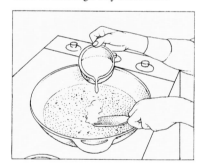

6 Lower the heat, stir in the cream and heat through. Taste and adjust seasoning, then pour over the chops. Garnish with tarragon and serve at once.

Menu Suggestion

Veal Chops in Wine is the perfect main course for a special dinner party. Serve with buttered noodles followed by a tomato and fresh fennel salad.

SWEDISH VEAL MEATBALLS

1.15* 🍲 £ £ ✳* 492 cals

*plus 1 hour chilling; freeze after step 5

Serves 4

450 g (1 lb) lean veal, pork or beef (or a mixture of these)

100 g (4 oz) smoked streaky bacon, rinded

½ small onion, skinned

50 g (2 oz) stale brown bread

2.5 ml (½ tsp) ground allspice

salt and freshly ground pepper

75 g (3 oz) unsalted butter

450 ml (¾ pint) chicken stock

juice of ½ lemon

10 ml (2 tsp) chopped fresh dill or 5 ml (1 tsp) dried

142 ml (5 fl oz) soured cream

dill sprigs, to garnish (optional)

1 Put the meat, bacon, onion and bread through the blades of a mincer twice so that they are minced very fine. (Or work them in a food processor.)

2 Add the allspice to the mixture with seasoning to taste, then mix in with the fingertips to bind the mixture. (Pick up a handful and press firmly in the hand—it should cling together, but not be too wet.) Chill in the refrigerator for 1 hour.

3 Melt the butter gently in a large flameproof casserole. Dip a tablespoon in the butter, then use to shape a spoonful of the minced mixture.

4 Add the meatball to the casserole and then continue dipping the spoon in the butter and shaping meatballs until there are 12–14 altogether.

5 Fry the meatballs half at a time, if necessary, over moderate heat until they are browned on all sides. Return all the meatballs to the casserole, pour in the stock and lemon juice and bring slowly to boiling point. Lower the heat, add the dill and seasoning to taste, then cover the casserole and simmer gently for 30 minutes.

6 Stir the soured cream into the casserole and mix gently to combine evenly with the meatballs and cooking liquid. Taste and adjust the seasoning of the sauce and then garnish with dill sprigs, if liked. Serve hot.

Menu Suggestion
In Sweden and other parts of Scandinavia, these meatballs are traditionally served with boiled potatoes and creamed spinach.

SWEDISH VEAL MEATBALLS

Egg-shaped meatballs like these are popular all over Scandinavia, where they are served for the evening meal with hot vegetables. Our version are casseroled, but they are often served simply fried in butter, with a gravy made from the pan juices. In Denmark, these are known as frikadeller, and are immensely popular. The Danes use minced pork to make them, and sometimes they add a little smoked bacon to the mixture, for extra flavour. Some Scandinavian cooks stir a little soda water into the meat mixture before it is shaped. If you have soda water to hand, you can add up to 45 ml (3 tbsp) for a lighter result.

Lamb

Lamb is often neglected as a casserole meat, and yet there is a huge variety of suitable cuts to choose from, most of which are extremely economical. From traditional recipes like Irish Stew and the French Navarin d'Agneau, to the more exotic Middle Eastern Tajine and the Indian Lamb Korma, this chapter is full of ideas for just about every occasion.

CREOLE LAMB

| 2.30 | 531–797 cals |

Serves 4–6

30 ml (2 tbsp) flour

15 ml (1 tbsp) ground turmeric

salt and freshly ground pepper

1.1 kg (2½ lb) boned lean shoulder of lamb, trimmed of fat and cubed

45 ml (3 tbsp) peanut or vegetable oil

2 onions, skinned and chopped

2 garlic cloves, skinned and chopped

450 g (1 lb) tomatoes, skinned and chopped or 396 g (14 oz) can

juice of 1 lime

225 g (8 oz) small, thin okra

15 ml (1 tbsp) chopped fresh coriander

sprig of coriander, to garnish

lemon and lime slices, to garnish

1 Mix together the flour, turmeric and seasoning in a polythene bag. Add the lamb in batches and shake the bag until the meat is evenly coated in the flour mixture.

2 Heat the oil in a large flame-proof casserole. Add lamb in batches and fry over brisk heat until browned on all sides. Remove with a slotted spoon and set aside.

3 Add the onions and garlic to the casserole and fry gently for 5 minutes until soft. Add the tomatoes and half the lime juice, then fry for a further few minutes, stirring to break up the tomatoes. Return the lamb to the casserole and bring slowly to boiling point.

4 Cover the casserole and cook in the oven at 170°C (325°F) mark 3 for 1½ hours.

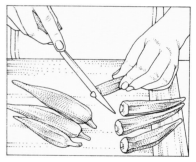

5 Meanwhile, prepare the okra. Wipe them, then cut off the top ends with a sharp knife. Do not pierce the flesh or the okra will burst open during cooking and spoil the appearance of the dish.

6 Add the okra to the casserole with half of the coriander and cook for a further 30 minutes or until the lamb is tender. Before serving, adjust seasoning, then sprinkle with the remaining lime juice and garnish with coriander and lemon and lime slices.

Menu Suggestion
Serve with plain boiled rice.

TAJINE
(SPICED LAMB AND FRUIT CASSEROLE)

| 1.45 | £ £ | 590–885 cals |

Serves 4–6

| 15 ml (1 tbsp) vegetable oil |
| 30 ml (2 tbsp) butter |
| 1.1 kg (2½ lb) boned leg of lamb, cubed |
| 1 onion, skinned and sliced |
| 5 ml (1 tsp) ground ginger |
| 5 ml (1 tsp) ground cinnamon |
| 1.25 ml (¼ tsp) powdered saffron |
| salt and freshly ground pepper |
| 225 g (8 oz) mixed dried fruit (e.g. prunes, apples, apricots, pears), soaked and stoned if necessary |
| 25 g (1 oz) sesame seeds, to garnish |

1 Heat the oil with the butter in a flameproof casserole. Add the lamb, onion, spices and seasoning and stir well to mix. Fry, stirring, over moderate heat until the meat cubes are browned on all sides.

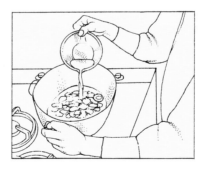

2 Pour enough water into the casserole to just cover the meat, then bring slowly to boiling point, stirring constantly.

3 Cover the casserole with a lid and simmer gently for 1 hour. Stir frequently during this time to prevent sticking.

4 Add the dried fruit and stir well to mix with the meat, then continue cooking for a further 30 minutes or until the lamb is tender and the liquid has reduced to a thick sauce.

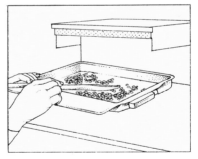

5 Meanwhile, spread the sesame seeds out evenly in a grill pan and toast them under a moderate grill until colouring. Shake pan constantly to avoid scorching.

6 When the lamb is tender, taste and adjust the seasoning. Transfer to a warmed serving dish, sprinkle with the toasted sesame seeds and serve at once.

Menu Suggestion
Serve this Middle Eastern dish with saffron rice and a yogurt and cucumber salad.

IRISH STEW

3.15*	£	367–550 cals

Serves 4–6

900 g (2 lb) scrag end of neck of lamb

1 kg (2¼ lb) potatoes, peeled and sliced

2 large onions, skinned and sliced

salt and freshly ground pepper

15 ml (1 tbsp) pearl barley

about 450 ml (¾ pint) chicken stock

chopped fresh parsley, to garnish

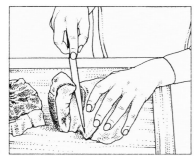

1 Using a sharp knife, divide meat into 8, then trim.

2 Place alternate layers of vegetables and meat in a saucepan, seasoning with salt and pepper. Finish with the pearl barley sprinkled over and a final layer of potatoes. Add sufficient stock to half cover.

3 Cover with a lid and simmer very slowly for about 3 hours. (Alternatively, cook the stew in a casserole in the oven at 190°C (375°F) mark 5 for 2½–3 hours.) Serve sprinkled with parsley.

Menu Suggestion

Traditional Irish stew, with meat and potatoes cooked together in the same pot, should be served with a simple vegetable such as carrots, peas or cabbage.

IRISH STEW

This recipe was originally intended for the toughest cuts of mutton and goat—the long, slow cooking made them tender and palatable, and their strong flavours mingled with herbs, onions and potatoes to produce a wonderfully aromatic dish. Nowadays, lamb is most often used—either scrag end as in this recipe, or best end, which is slightly more expensive but not quite so fatty. If using scrag end, ask the butcher to chop it into serving pieces for you if you wish, as the bones are quite difficult to cut yourself at home. Best end is sold as chops, therefore no cutting is required.

NAVARIN D'AGNEAU
(SPRING LAMB CASSEROLE)

| 2.10 | £ ✳* | 771 cals |

* freeze after step 4 without adding the potatoes

Serves 4

30 ml (2 tbsp) vegetable oil

1 kg (2¼ lb) best end of neck of lamb, divided into cutlets

5 ml (1 tsp) sugar plus a little extra

15 ml (1 tbsp) plain flour

900 ml (1½ pints) chicken stock

30 ml (2 tbsp) tomato purée

salt and freshly ground pepper

bouquet garni

225 g (8 oz) button onions, skinned

4 carrots, peeled and sliced

1–2 turnips, peeled and quartered

8 small even-sized potatoes, peeled

225 g (8 oz) fresh peas, shelled, or 112 g (4 oz) packet frozen peas

chopped fresh parsley, to garnish

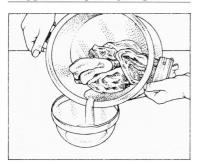

1 Heat the oil in a saucepan and fry the cutlets for about 5 minutes on both sides until lightly browned. If there is too much fat at this stage, pour off a little to leave 15–30 ml (1–2 tbsp).

2 Stir in 5 ml (1 tsp) sugar and heat until it browns slightly, then add the flour, stirring all the time until cooked and browned.

3 Remove from the heat, stir in the stock gradually, then bring to the boil and add the tomato purée, seasoning, a pinch of sugar and the bouquet garni. Cover, reduce the heat and simmer for about 1 hour.

4 Remove the bouquet garni, add the onions, carrots and turnips and continue cooking for 30 minutes. Add the potatoes and cook for 10 minutes more.

5 Stir in the peas and cook for a further 10 minutes or until the meat and potatoes are tender.

6 To serve, place the meat on a warmed serving dish and surround with the vegetables. Garnish with parsley.

Menu Suggestion

Hot French bread is the traditional accompaniment to this classic French stew of meat and vegetables cooked together.

NAVARIN D'AGNEAU

This French casserole was originally made with mutton — and so called Navarin de Mouton. These days, mutton is almost impossible to come by, and so lamb is invariably used instead. It is a classic springtime dish, which should be made with freshly picked, young spring vegetables, although frozen peas and beans are often used for convenience at other times of year.

LAMB KORMA

2.15	✳	348 cals

Serves 4

2 onions, skinned and chopped

2.5 cm (1 inch) piece fresh root ginger, peeled

40 g (1½ oz) blanched almonds

2 garlic cloves, skinned

90 ml (6 tbsp) water

5 ml (1 tsp) ground cardamom

5 ml (1 tsp) ground cloves

5 ml (1 tsp) ground cinnamon

5 ml (1 tsp) ground cumin

5 ml (1 tsp) ground coriander

1.25 ml (¼ tsp) cayenne pepper

45 ml (3 tbsp) vegetable oil or ghee

900 g (2 lb) boned tender lamb, cubed

300 ml (½ pint) natural yogurt

salt and freshly ground pepper

cucumber and lime slices, to garnish

1 Put the onions, ginger, almonds and garlic in a blender or food processor with the water and blend to a smooth paste. Add the spices and mix well.

2 Heat the oil or ghee in a heavy-based saucepan and fry the lamb for 5 minutes until browned on all sides.

3 Add the paste mixture and fry for about 10 minutes, stirring, until the mixture is lightly browned. Stir in the yogurt 15 ml (1 tbsp) at a time and season.

4 Cover with a tight-fitting lid, reduce the heat and simmer for 1¼–1½ hours or until the meat is really tender.

5 Transfer to a warmed serving dish and serve garnished with cucumber and lime slices.

Menu Suggestion

Serve with plain boiled or pilau rice, poppadoms, cucumber and yogurt raita, and a sag aloo (spinach and potato curry).

LAMB KORMA

Mild in flavour, creamy in texture, the Indian korma is a very special dish, which was originally only served on special occasions such as feast days and holidays. Our version is relatively simple compared with some of the korma recipes which were devised for celebrations. These often contained such luxurious ingredients as saffron (the most expensive spice in the world), cashew nuts and double cream. If you want to make a richer korma for a dinner party main course, then add powdered saffron or infused saffron liquid with the ground spices in step 1, and stir in 50 g (2 oz) chopped unsalted cashew nuts just before serving. Substitute double cream for the yogurt and swirl more cream over the top of the korma before garnishing.

MIDDLE EASTERN MEATBALLS WITH AUBERGINE AND TOMATO

| 1.30* | | ✳ | 415 cals |

* plus 30 minutes degorging aubergines and 1 hour chilling

Serves 6

2 medium aubergines, about 450 g
  (1 lb) total weight, sliced

salt and freshly ground pepper

150 ml (¼ pint) vegetable oil

450 g (1 lb) boneless lamb

2 thick slices of white bread,
  crusts removed

1 small onion, skinned

10 ml (2 tsp) ground cumin

450 g (1 lb) tomatoes, skinned and
  chopped

15 ml (1 tbsp) tomato purée

450 ml (¾ pint) chicken stock or dry
  white wine and water, mixed

2.5 ml (½ tsp) ground allspice

450 ml (¾ pint) vegetable oil, for
  deep-frying

chopped fresh parsley, to serve

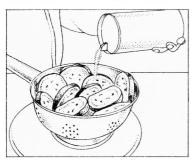

1 Layer the aubergine slices in a colander, sprinkling each layer with salt. Cover with a plate, weight down and leave for 30 minutes to draw out moisture.

2 Drain the aubergine slices, rinse and dry well. In a large frying pan, fry for 4–5 minutes in batches in the oil, turning once. Drain the fried aubergines on absorbent kitchen paper.

3 Put the lamb through the blades of a mincer twice with the fried aubergines, bread and onion. (Or work the ingredients in a food processor.)

4 In a bowl, mix the minced meat with the cumin and seasoning to taste, then chill in the refrigerator for about 30 minutes, until firm.

5 Meanwhile, put the tomatoes, tomato purée, stock and allspice in a large flameproof casserole with seasoning to taste. Bring to the boil, stirring to break up the tomatoes, then lower the heat and simmer while making the meatballs.

6 With floured hands, form the mixture into 30 walnut-sized balls. Chill in the refrigerator for 30 minutes to firm.

7 Heat the oil for deep-frying to 190°C (375°F). Add the meatballs in batches and fry until browned on all sides. Remove with a slotted spoon and drain on absorbent kitchen paper.

8 Add the drained meatballs to the tomato sauce then cover and simmer gently for 30 minutes, shaking the casserole frequently so that the meatballs become saturated in the sauce.

9 Taste and, if necessary, adjust the seasoning of the tomato sauce before serving. Garnish with chopped fresh parsley.

Menu Suggestion
Serve with boiled basmati rice as part of a Middle Eastern style meal. Start with hot pitta bread and taramasalata or houmos, and finish with a fresh fruit salad.

MIDDLE EASTERN MEATBALLS

Lamb, aubergines and tomatoes are a popular combination of ingredients in Middle Eastern cookery. Here the lamb and aubergines are minced together to make meatballs, an unusual method, but one which gives a tasty, moist result. To save time, buy ready-minced lamb, but make sure it is fairly lean, or the fat will run out into the sauce and make the dish unpalatable.

GREEK LAMB

| 2.20 | ✳ | 673–1011 cals |

Serves 4–6

60 ml (4 tbsp) olive oil

900 g (2 lb) small new potatoes, scraped, or old potatoes, peeled and cut into cubes

1.1 kg (2½ lb) boned lean shoulder of lamb, trimmed of fat and cubed

2 large onions, skinned and sliced

15 ml (1 tbsp) plain flour

300 ml (½ pint) dry white wine

350 g (12 oz) tomatoes, skinned and chopped

30 ml (2 tbsp) wine vinegar

2 cinnamon sticks

2 bay leaves

10 ml (2 tsp) chopped fresh thyme or 5 ml (1 tsp) dried

salt and freshly ground pepper

thyme sprigs, to garnish

1 Heat 30 ml (2 tbsp) of the oil in a large flameproof casserole. Pierce each potato (or potato cube) with a sharp knife, add to the casserole and fry over moderate heat until golden on all sides. Remove from the oil with a slotted spoon and drain on absorbent kitchen paper.

2 Heat the remaining oil in the casserole, add the lamb and onions in batches and fry over moderate heat until browned on all sides. Sprinkle in the flour and fry 1 further minute, stirring until it is absorbed.

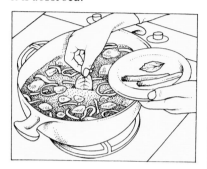

3 Pour the wine into the casserole and add the tomatoes and wine vinegar. Bring slowly to boiling point, then lower the heat and add the cinnamon, bay leaves, thyme and seasoning to taste. Cover and simmer gently for 1 hour, stirring occasionally.

4 Add the fried potatoes to the casserole and continue simmering for 1 further hour or until the lamb and potatoes are tender. Remove the cinnamon sticks and bay leaves, then taste and adjust seasoning. Garnish with thyme sprigs and serve the casserole immediately.

Menu Suggestion
Serve with a Greek-style salad of tomato, shredded white cabbage, raw onion, black olives and chopped fresh coriander.

GREEK LAMB

A rich and pungent dish, Greek Lamb is given its authentic flavour with the combination of olive oil, white wine, tomatoes, cinnamon and fresh thyme. Greek olive oil from the first cold pressing of the olives is thick and green, often with flecks of olives floating in it. Look for it in Greek and Cypriot food shops—its superb flavour and texture make it good for salads as well as cooking.

MARINATED LEG OF LAMB

| 2.15* | £ £ | ✳* | 430–645 cals |

* plus 24 hours marinating; freeze in the marinade

Serves 4–6

1.8 kg (4 lb) leg of lamb

2 garlic cloves, skinned and cut into slivers

few rosemary sprigs

salt and freshly ground pepper

90 ml (6 tbsp) olive oil

30 ml (2 tbsp) lemon juice

30 ml (2 tbsp) white wine vinegar

150 ml ($\frac{1}{4}$ pint) dry white wine or water

extra rosemary sprigs, to garnish

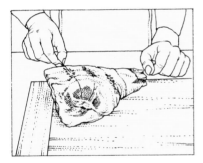

1 Make deep incisions in the lamb with a sharp, pointed knife. Insert the slivers of garlic and the sprigs of rosemary into the incisions.

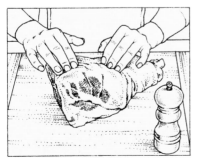

2 Rub the outside of the joint all over with plenty of salt and freshly ground pepper.

3 Mix together the oil, lemon juice and wine vinegar, then brush all over the joint. Place the joint in a flameproof casserole and leave to marinate for 24 hours.

4 Put the casserole on top of the cooker and fry the joint over moderate heat until browned on all sides. Pour in the wine or water, bring slowly to boiling point, then cover and simmer gently for 2 hours or until the lamb is very tender, basting occasionally. Serve hot, garnished with fresh rosemary sprigs.

Menu Suggestion

This French-style casserole makes an unusual Sunday lunch. Serve with new potatoes tossed in melted butter and chopped fresh mint, and a selection of fresh seasonal vegetables such as carrots, courgettes and beans.

MARINATED LEG OF LAMB

Freezing meat in a marinade is a convenient way to impart flavour, which involves little or no effort on your part! Simply place the leg of lamb in a rigid container and follow the recipe instructions above up to step 3. Instead of leaving to marinate in a cool place for 24 hours, seal the container and freeze for up to 6 months. Defrost at room temperature overnight, then continue from the beginning of step 4—nothing could be simpler!

SPICED LAMB WITH SPINACH

1.20*	533 cals

* plus 4 hours marinating
Serves 4

900 g (2 lb) boned leg or shoulder of lamb, trimmed of fat and cubed

90 ml (6 tbsp) natural yogurt

1 cm ($\frac{1}{2}$ inch) piece fresh root ginger, peeled and chopped

2 garlic cloves, skinned and chopped

2.5 cm (1 inch) cinnamon stick

2 bay leaves

2 green cardamoms

4 black peppercorns

3 whole cloves

5 ml (1 tsp) ground cumin

5 ml (1 tsp) garam masala

1.25–2.5 ml ($\frac{1}{4}$–$\frac{1}{2}$ tsp) chilli powder

5 ml (1 tsp) ground coriander

5 ml (1 tsp) salt

450 g (1 lb) fresh or 225 g (8 oz) frozen spinach

sprig of mint and lemon slices, to garnish

1 Place the cubes of meat in a bowl. Then, in a separate bowl, mix together the yogurt, ginger, garlic, whole and ground spices and the salt.

2 Spoon the mixture over the meat and mix thoroughly. Cover and leave to marinate at room temperature for about 4 hours.

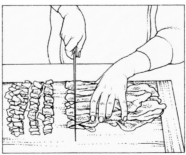

3 Meanwhile, thoroughly wash and chop the fresh spinach. Thaw frozen spinach in a pan.

4 Put the marinated meat in a heavy-based saucepan and cook over a low heat for about 1 hour, stirring occasionally, until all the moisture has evaporated and the meat is tender.

5 Stir in the spinach and cook over low heat for a further 10 minutes. Serve garnished with mint and lemon slices.

Menu Suggestion
Spicy and rich, this Indian dish of lamb and spinach goes well with plain boiled basmati rice. Serve cucumber raita and mango chutney as side dishes.

POT ROAST LAMB WITH WINTER VEGETABLES

| 3.00 | 442–590 cals |

Serves 6–8

| 15 ml (1 tbsp) vegetable oil |
| 1.6 kg (3½ lb) leg of lamb |
| 3 onions, skinned and quartered |
| 4 carrots, peeled and thickly sliced |
| 2 leeks, sliced and washed |
| 30 ml (2 tbsp) tomato purée |
| 396 g (14 oz) can tomatoes |
| 1 garlic clove, skinned and crushed |
| bouquet garni |
| salt and freshly ground pepper |

1 Heat the oil in a large frying pan and fry the joint of meat on all sides for about 10 minutes until browned. Remove meat and place in a large casserole.

2 Add the onions, carrots and leeks to frying pan and fry for 5 minutes, stirring occasionally. Remove from pan, then arrange around the lamb. Stir in the tomato purée with the tomatoes and their juice. Add the garlic, bouquet garni and seasoning.

3 Cover and cook in the oven at 170°C (325°F) mark 3 for about 2½ hours or until the meat is tender.

4 Discard the bouquet garni. Transfer the lamb to a warmed serving dish and surround with the vegetables.

5 Skim as much fat as possible from the liquid in the casserole, and serve separately in a sauceboat.

Menu Suggestion
An unusual alternative to roast lamb for Sunday lunch. Serve with jacket baked potatoes and a seasonal green vegetable.

Pork and Bacon

Rich and tasty, pork and bacon make sumptuous casserole dishes, and combine beautifully with other ingredients, especially tangy citrus fruits and the strong flavours of chillies, peppers and ginger. This chapter includes recipes from Britain, France and Italy, as well as several from as far afield as China and the Far East. Whichever you choose to try, you are bound to be delighted with the results.

PORK AND BEAN STEW

| 2.30* | £ | 345–518 cals |

* plus overnight soaking for the beans

Serves 4–6

450 g (1 lb) lean belly pork

225 g (8 oz) dried black-eye or haricot beans, soaked overnight in cold water

15 ml (1 tbsp) black treacle

900 ml (1½ pints) chicken stock

1 onion, skinned and stuck with a few whole cloves

bouquet garni

3 medium carrots, peeled and sliced

2 leeks, trimmed and sliced

30 ml (2 tbsp) Worcestershire sauce

15 ml (1 tbsp) tomato purée

salt and freshly ground pepper

1 Cut the pork into chunky cubes, removing the rind and any bones. Fry in a flameproof casserole over brisk heat until the fat runs.

2 Drain the beans and add to the pork with the treacle, stock, onion and bouquet garni. Bring slowly to boiling point, then lower the heat, cover and simmer for 1½ hours or until the beans are just becoming tender.

3 Add the carrots and leeks to the casserole, with the Worcestershire sauce, tomato purée and seasoning to taste. Continue cooking for a further 30 minutes or until the beans are really tender. Discard the bouquet garni and taste and adjust seasoning before serving.

Menu Suggestion

Hot garlic or herb bread is the only accompaniment needed for this substantial stew. Ice-cold lager or beer is a suitable drink.

PORK AND BEAN STEW

An anglicised version of the famous American dish Boston Baked Beans, this Pork and Bean Stew is a most economical way to feed as many as six people with hearty appetites. Don't worry about the small quantity of meat, because pulses are extremely nutritious: they're packed with protein, iron and vitamins (especially those from the B group), plus the fact that they're extremely low in fat compared with other high-protein foods — yet very high in fibre.

Black-eye beans, sometimes also called black-eyed peas, are so called because of the characteristic black spot on their sides. They add interest to this casserole because of their unusual looks, although the more common haricot beans (the ones that are used to make canned baked beans) may be used just as well.

SWEET AND SOUR SPARE RIB CHOPS

1.15* ✳* 372 cals

* plus 4 hours marinating; freeze in the marinade before cooking

Serves 4

30 ml (2 tbsp) wine vinegar
30 ml (2 tbsp) soy sauce
30 ml (2 tbsp) soft brown sugar
15 ml (1 tbsp) Worcestershire sauce
5 ml (1 tsp) garlic salt
1.25 ml ($\frac{1}{4}$ tsp) chilli powder
4 spare rib pork chops (see box)
45 ml (3 tbsp) vegetable oil
300 ml ($\frac{1}{2}$ pint) chicken stock or water
1 small bunch of spring onions, to finish

1 Make the marinade. Mix the first six ingredients together in a shallow dish. Add the chops and turn to coat, then cover and leave to marinate for 4 hours. Turn the chops in the marinade occasionally during this time.

2 Remove the chops from the marinade. Heat 30 ml (2 tbsp) of the oil in a flameproof casserole, which is large enough to hold the chops in a single layer. Add the chops and fry over brisk heat until browned on all sides.

3 Mix the marinade with the stock or water, then pour over the chops. Bring slowly to boiling point, then lower the heat, cover and simmer gently for 45 minutes or until the chops are tender.

4 Ten minutes before serving, chop the spring onions, reserving the tops for the garnish. Heat the remaining oil in a small pan, add the chopped onions and fry gently for a few minutes until softened. Sprinkle over the dish just before serving and garnish with the reserved tops.

Menu Suggestion
Serve these spare rib chops for an informal supper party with a medley of fried rice, diced pepper and spring onions. Follow with a mixed salad.

SWEET AND SOUR SPARE RIB CHOPS
Take care to buy the right cut of pork for this recipe. Spare rib chops are from the neck end of the pig; thick and meaty, they become succulent and tender when casseroled, and yet they are inexpensive to buy compared with the leaner loin chops, that are better suited to a quick-cooking method such as grilling. Do not confuse spare rib chops with spare ribs, which are cut from inside the thick end of the belly—these are the kind used in Chinese cookery, most often served in a sweet and sour sauce.

CHILLI PORK

| 1.00* | £ £ ✳* | 879 cals |

* plus at least 4 hours marinating;
freeze after step 4

Serves 4

900 g (2 lb) pork fillets (tenderloin)

45 ml (3 tbsp) soy sauce

15 ml (1 tbsp) hoisin sauce (see box)

15 ml (1 tbsp) soft brown sugar

30 ml (2 tbsp) crushed fresh root ginger or 10 ml (2 tsp) ground

60 ml (4 tbsp) vegetable oil

15 ml (1 tbsp) crushed dried red chillies, or less, according to taste

150 ml (¼ pint) chicken stock or water

10 ml (2 tsp) cornflour

350 g (12 oz) long-grain rice, boiled, to serve

few sliced red chillies, to garnish

1 Place the pork fillets in a shallow dish. Mix together the next four ingredients with half of the oil and pour over the pork. Cover and leave to marinate for at least 4 hours.

2 Heat the remaining oil in a flameproof casserole, add crushed chillies to taste and fry gently for 5 minutes, stirring all the time.

3 Remove the pork fillets from the marinade and add to the casserole. Fry over moderate heat, turning constantly until browned on all sides.

4 Mix the marinade with the stock or water, then pour over the pork. Bring slowly to boiling point, then lower the heat, cover and simmer for 45 minutes or until the pork is tender. Baste the pork frequently during the cooking time.

5 To serve, remove the pork from the cooking liquid and place on a board. Mix the cornflour to a paste with a little water, then stir into the cooking liquid and bring to the boil. Simmer, stirring, until the sauce thickens.

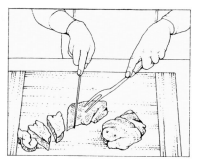

6 Carve the pork neatly into thin diagonal slices. Spread the hot boiled rice out on a warmed serving platter, arrange the pork slices on top and spoon over some of the sauce. Garnish with sliced chillies and serve, with the remaining sauce handed separately.

Menu Suggestion
Spicy and hot, Chilli Pork is served with boiled rice. Follow with a cooling green salad of shredded lettuce, cucumber and celery.

CHILLI PORK

This recipe for Chilli Pork is similar to the Chinese 'Red-Cooked Pork' and the Burmese 'Red Pork' or 'Wet-thani'. Such dishes are immensely popular in Eastern and Oriental cookery, where chillies are used both as a flavouring and colouring. Dried red chillies are easy to obtain in Oriental and Asian stores, but if you are unable to buy them, then you can use chilli powder instead. For this recipe, use 5 ml (1 tsp) chilli powder, as the flavour should be hot and strong, although different brands of chilli powder vary in their strength, so it is best to taste before serving in case more needs to be added. Hoisin sauce, also called hosin sauce and sometimes Chinese barbecue sauce, is sold in Chinese supermarkets. Available in cans and jars, it keeps for months in the refrigerator once opened, and can be used in numerous Chinese dishes. Made from soya beans, flour, sugar and spices, it helps give this dish its characteristic red colour.

PORK CHOPS IN ORANGE JUICE

1.00	✳*	395 cals

* freeze after step 5

Serves 4

30 ml (2 tbsp) plain flour, for coating

2.5 ml ($\frac{1}{2}$ tsp) ground mixed spice

salt and freshly ground pepper

4 loin pork chops, trimmed of rind and fat

15 g ($\frac{1}{2}$ oz) butter

30 ml (2 tbsp) vegetable oil

1 medium onion, skinned and chopped

half 170 ml (6 fl oz) can frozen concentrated orange juice

Tabasco sauce, to taste

1 bay leaf

30–45 ml (2–3 tbsp) shredded orange rind, to garnish

1 Place the flour in a bowl. Add the spice and seasoning. Dip the chops in the seasoned flour, ensuring that they are evenly coated on both sides.

2 Melt the butter with the oil in a large flameproof casserole. Add the chops and fry over moderate heat until browned on all sides. Remove from the casserole with a slotted spoon and drain on absorbent kitchen paper.

3 Add the onion to the casserole with any flour remaining from the chops and fry gently for 5 minutes until onion is soft but not coloured.

4 Dilute the orange juice with 200 ml (7 fl oz) water, then pour into the casserole and stir to combine with the onion.

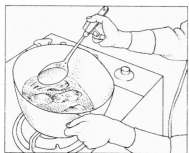

5 Return the chops to the casserole and bring slowly to boiling point. Lower heat, add bay leaf and Tabasco to taste. Cover and simmer for 45 minutes until the chops are tender. Baste occasionally during this time.

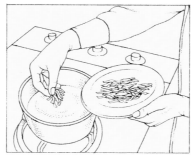

6 A few minutes before the end of the cooking time, blanch the orange rind for 1 minute in boiling water. Drain, rinse under cold running water (to preserve a good colour), then dry on absorbent kitchen paper.

7 Transfer the chops to a warmed serving dish, then remove the bay leaf and taste and adjust the seasoning of the orange sauce. Pour the sauce over the chops, sprinkle with the blanched orange rind and serve at once.

Menu Suggestion
A colourful, fruity main course for a dinner party. Serve with buttered noodles and a crisp green salad or seasonal green vegetable.

CHINESE PORK AND GINGER CASSEROLE

| 1.25 | ✳* | 448 cals |

* freeze after step 4

Serves 4

30 ml (2 tbsp) vegetable oil

1 small onion, skinned and finely chopped

2.5 cm (1 inch) piece fresh root ginger

700 g (1½ lb) boneless lean pork (e.g. shoulder or sparerib), cubed

30 ml (2 tbsp) dry sherry

15 ml (1 tbsp) soy sauce

300 ml (½ pint) dry or American ginger ale

2.5 ml (½ tsp) five-spice powder

salt and freshly ground pepper

50 g (2 oz) stem ginger, sliced

½ red pepper, cored, seeded and sliced

½ yellow pepper, cored, seeded and sliced

1 Heat the oil in a flameproof casserole, add the onion and fry gently for 5 minutes until soft but not coloured.

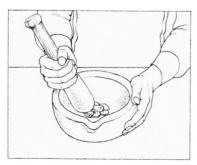

2 Meanwhile, skin the root ginger and then crush the flesh with a mortar and pestle.

3 Add the crushed ginger to the casserole with the pork, increase the heat and fry until the meat is browned on all sides.

4 Stir in the sherry and soy sauce, then the ginger ale, five-spice powder and seasoning to taste. Bring slowly to boiling point, stirring, then lower the heat, cover and simmer for about 1 hour until the pork is just tender.

5 Add the stem ginger and pepper slices to the casserole and continue cooking for a further 10 minutes. Serve hot.

Menu Suggestion

An informal supper party dish. Serve with Chinese egg noodles and stir-fried vegetables such as grated carrots, finely sliced celery, green pepper and beansprouts.

PORK IN CIDER

| 2.15 | 580–870 cals |

Serves 4–6

1.1 kg (2½ lb) boned and rolled lean
  shoulder or hand of pork, rind
  and excess fat removed

2 garlic cloves, skinned and cut
  into slivers

30 ml (2 tbsp) vegetable oil

salt and freshly ground pepper

300 ml (½ pint) dry cider

about 350 g (12 oz) white cabbage

1 large cooking apple

25 g (1 oz) butter

1 onion, skinned and sliced

5 ml (1 tsp) caraway seeds

paprika, to garnish (optional)

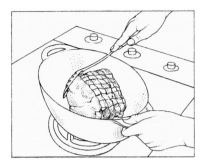

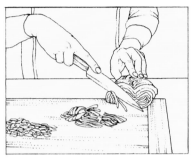

1 With a sharp, pointed knife, make deep incisions in the pork. Insert the garlic slivers, pushing them down into the meat.

2 Heat the oil in a large flame-proof casserole, add the pork and fry over moderate heat until browned on all sides. Sprinkle with salt and pepper, then pour in the cider and bring very slowly to boiling point.

3 Cover the casserole and cook in the oven at 170°C (325°F) mark 3 for 1½ hours.

4 Meanwhile, shred the cabbage, cutting away all thick, coarse stalks. Peel and core the apple, then slice it thickly.

5 Melt the butter in a saucepan, add the cabbage and apple and fry gently for 5 minutes, tossing the mixture constantly. Stir in the caraway seeds.

6 Add the cabbage mixture to the casserole, stirring it into the cooking liquid around the pork. Continue cooking for a further 30 minutes or until the pork is tender. Taste and adjust the seasoning of the cabbage and sauce before serving. Garnish the cabbage with paprika, if liked.

Menu Suggestion

Pork in Cider is ideal for a family weekend lunch. Serve with contrasting colourful vegetables such as carrots and broccoli. Roast potatoes can also be served if liked.

PORK IN CIDER

This combination of pork, apples, cider and cabbage is popular in the Alsace region of north-eastern France, where it is simply called Porc Alsacienne. Alsatian cider is strong and dry and gives this dish a unique, heady flavour. French dry cider is now available in many supermarkets and off licences, and is well worth seeking out if you are keen for this dish to have an authentic flavour.

ITALIAN-STYLE BRAISED PORK

| 2.00 | 450 cals |

Serves 6

15 ml (1 tbsp) vegetable oil

25 g (1 oz) butter

1 kg (2¼ lb) loin of pork, rinded

2 garlic cloves, skinned

1 large onion, skinned and chopped

568 ml (1 pint) milk

5 juniper berries

2 rosemary sprigs, plus extra for garnish

salt and freshly ground pepper

1 Heat the oil and the butter in a large saucepan or flameproof casserole into which the meat will just fit and fry the pork, garlic and onion for about 15 minutes until the pork is browned on all sides. Add the milk, juniper berries, rosemary and seasoning.

2 Bring to the boil, cover, turn the heat down and cook for 1½–2 hours until the pork is tender, turning and basting from time to time.

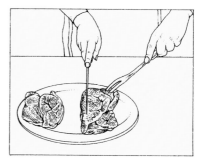

3 Transfer the pork to a warmed serving dish and carve into thick slices. Discard the garlic, juniper berries and rosemary. The milky cooking juices will look curdled, so rub the sauce through a sieve or liquidise in a blender or food processor until smooth. Taste and adjust the seasoning. Pour a little of the sauce over the slices and serve the remaining sauce separately. Garnish with sprigs of rosemary.

Menu Suggestion
Rich and tender, this casserole of pork braised in milk tastes good with steamed or boiled new potatoes, and a green salad tossed in a sharp oil and vinegar dressing.

ITALIAN-STYLE BRAISED PORK

Cooking pork in milk may seem a very strange combination at first, but it is very popular in Italy. The milk and the long, slow cooking produce the most tender results, making Arrosto di Maiale al Latte, as the Italians call this dish, a firm favourite for Sunday lunches, even with the less tender cuts of pork. The loin used in this recipe is a tender, expensive, cut of pork, but it can be rather dry if roasted in the normal way, because it is so lean. Braising loin of pork in milk ensures that the meat will be moist and succulent, and the flavour of garlic, juniper and rosemary gives the dish a unique aromatic taste.

BACON HOT POT

| 2.45 | £ | 335–502 cals |

Serves 4–6

700 g (1½ lb) unsmoked collar or
   slipper joint of bacon

900 g (2 lb) potatoes

1 small onion, skinned and thinly
   sliced

2 cooking apples, peeled, cored and
   thickly sliced

10 ml (2 tsp) chopped fresh sage or
   5 ml (1 tsp) dried

salt and freshly ground pepper

150 ml (¼ pint) natural
   unsweetened apple juice

150 ml (¼ pint) water

15 g (½ oz) unsalted butter

15 ml (1 tbsp) vegetable oil

1 Remove the rind and excess fat
from the bacon and cut the
bacon into bite-sized pieces. Put
the pieces in a saucepan, cover
with cold water and bring to the
boil. Drain thoroughly.

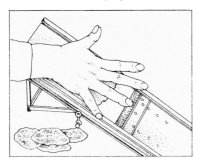

2 Peel the potatoes and slice
them thinly, using a mandolin
slicer if available.

3 Put the bacon, potatoes, onion
and apples in a shallow ovenproof casserole, sprinkling each
layer with sage and seasoning to
taste. (Take care not to add too
much salt because the bacon is
already salty.) Finish with a layer
of potatoes.

4 Mix together the apple juice
and water, then pour slowly
into the casserole. Cover and cook
in the oven at 180°C (350°F) mark
4 for 1½ hours.

5 Melt the butter with the oil in
a small pan. Uncover the
casserole and brush the top potato
layer with the melted fat. Return
to the oven and cook uncovered
for a further 30 minutes or until
the potatoes are golden brown.
Serve hot.

Menu Suggestion
Serve for a midweek supper with a
seasonal vegetable such as spinach,
peas or carrots.

WILTSHIRE GAMMON CASSEROLE

| 1.30* | 378–504 cals |

* plus 4 hours marinating and several hours cooling time if serving cold

Serves 6–8

1.4 kg (3 lb) unsmoked middle gammon joint, soaked for 4 hours in cold water (see box)

½ bottle rosé wine

10 ml (2 tsp) demerara sugar

few whole cloves

bouquet garni

1 Drain the joint, rinse under cold running water and then put into a casserole or saucepan into which it just fits. Mix together the wine, sugar and cloves in a separate pan and bring to just below boiling point.

2 Pour the hot liquid over the gammon, then tuck in the bouquet garni. Cover with a tight-fitting lid and leave to marinate for 4 hours. Turn the gammon in the marinade occasionally during this time.

3 Place the casserole on top of the cooker and bring slowly to boiling point. Lower the heat and simmer, covered, for 1 hour 20 minutes until the gammon is tender. Remove bouquet garni.

4 Cut into slices and serve hot, with a little of the cooking liquid spooned over. Alternatively, to serve cold, remove the gammon from the liquid and leave to cool for several hours before slicing. Serve with Cumberland sauce.

Menu Suggestion

If serving hot, sauté potatoes and a green salad would make ideal accompaniments. If serving cold, serve with a selection of salads.

WILTSHIRE GAMMON

Gammon is the name given to whole hind legs of bacon, cut after curing. The middle gammon specified in this recipe is the prime, central cut — whole middle gammons can weigh as much as 4 kg (9 lb), but these are usually cut into smaller joints which are of a more manageable size. For this recipe, try to get a mild Wiltshire or a tendersweet cure. Wiltshire cure means that the pork will have been injected with a brine solution, then immersed in brine for 2–4 days and afterwards left to hang in a maturing room if it is to be sold as unsmoked. With such mild cures of bacon, soaking in cold water before cooking is now considered unnecessary because the salt content is so low, but if you feel happier soaking the joint beforehand then by all means do so. Do not soak for longer than 4 hours, however, or the soaking will have the opposite of the desired effect — the salt which has come out of the joint into the soaking water will work its way back into the gammon, making it saltier than it was originally!

Sausages and Variety Meats

Not always the most popular choice for family meals, offal (or variety meats as they are now often called) responds well to the slow, moist cooking method of casseroling, and this chapter illustrates beautifully how the different kinds of offal can be cooked to their best advantage. Inexpensive and nutritious, offal always deserves a place in family menus, and the recipes in this chapter have been chosen especially with this in mind.

LIVER WITH SAGE AND MADEIRA

| 1.30 | £ | 409 cals |

Serves 4

450 g (1 lb) lamb's liver, sliced

salt and freshly ground pepper

25 g (1 oz) plain flour

25 g (1 oz) butter

45 ml (3 tbsp) vegetable oil

100 g (4 oz) mushrooms, wiped and sliced

1 garlic clove, skinned and crushed

5 ml (1 tsp) chopped fresh sage or 2.5 ml (½ tsp) dried

450 g (1 lb) tomatoes, skinned and chopped, or 397 g (14 oz) can tomatoes

45 ml (3 tbsp) Madeira (see box)

chicken stock, if necessary

sage leaves, to garnish

1 Dust the liver with seasoned flour, reserving the excess flour. Heat the butter and oil in a frying pan and quickly brown the liver on both sides. Transfer meat to a casserole.

2 Fry the mushrooms and garlic in the remaining fat for 5 minutes, then add to the casserole.

3 Add any remaining flour to the pan and mix well. Stir in the sage, tomatoes with their juice and Madeira. Bring to the boil, stirring, and pour over the liver mixture. Add a little stock, if necessary, to cover the liver.

4 Cover and cook in the oven at 170°C (325°F) mark 3 for about 1¼ hours until tender. Serve garnished with sage leaves.

Menu Suggestion

An excellent main course for a special family dinner, Liver with Sage and Madeira goes well with a plain accompaniment such as buttered tagliatelle, and a green vegetable.

LIVER WITH SAGE AND MADEIRA

The addition of Madeira to this recipe for lamb's liver, mushrooms and tomatoes turns it into a dish for a special occasion, but if you do not have Madeira you can equally well use sweet sherry or port instead.

Madeira has long been regarded as just a dessert wine, but there are four different types, two of which are actually dry and make excellent aperitifs if served chilled. All Madeiras are made in much the same way as sherry, but they also undergo a heating process after fermentation, which gives them their characteristic 'burnt' flavour. The darkest Madeira—and the sweetest and best-known—is Malmsey, which makes a rich and heady after-dinner drink; Bual is slightly less sweet and paler than Malmsey; Verdelho is drier, but not so dry as Sercial, which has quite a sharp tang.

LIVER WITH ORANGE

0.40 £ | 470 cals

Serves 4

3 oranges
300 ml (½ pint) boiling water
45 ml (3 tbsp) vegetable oil
1 onion, skinned and chopped
1 garlic clove, skinned and crushed
700 g (1½ lb) lamb's liver
salt and freshly ground pepper
45 ml (3 tbsp) plain flour
175 g (6 oz) mushrooms, sliced
fresh chervil, to garnish

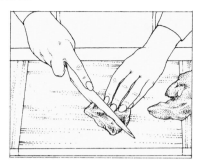

1 Thinly peel one of the oranges. Cut peel into thin strips and blanch in the 300 ml (½ pint) boiling water for 1 minute. Drain, reserving the peel and water. Squeeze the juice from the remaining oranges.

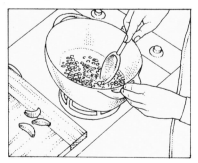

2 Heat the oil in a flameproof casserole and fry the onion and garlic for 5 minutes until golden.

3 Slice the liver and coat in seasoned flour. Add to the casserole and fry for 3 minutes until browned.

4 Make up the squeezed orange juice to 425 ml (14 fl oz) with the reserved blanching water. Add to the casserole with the mushrooms and seasoning.

5 Bring to the boil, stirring. Cover, reduce the heat and simmer gently for 20 minutes until tender. Garnish the liver with the blanched peel and chervil just before serving.

Menu Suggestion
Serve Liver with Orange for a family meal with creamed potatoes and a green vegetable such as petits pois or sliced courgettes.

LIVER WITH ORANGE
There are two reasons for blanching the orange peel in this recipe. The obvious reason is that the peel softens and therefore becomes more palatable as a garnish; blanching also helps retain the colour of citrus peel, especially if it is plunged into ice-cold water immediately after draining. Take care not to include any of the white pith when removing the peel from the orange as it tastes bitter.

BRAISED OXTAIL

| 4.30 | £ | ✳ | 256 cals |

Serves 4

2 small oxtails cut up, about 1.4 kg
   (3 lb) total weight
30 ml (2 tbsp) plain flour
salt and freshly ground pepper
40 g (1½ oz) lard
350 g (12 oz) onions, skinned and
   sliced
900 ml (1½ pints) beef stock
150 ml (¼ pint) red wine
15 ml (1 tbsp) tomato purée
pared rind of ½ lemon
2 bay leaves
225 g (8 oz) carrots, peeled and
   thickly sliced
450 g (1 lb) parsnips, peeled and cut
   into chunks
chopped fresh parsley, to garnish

1 Coat the oxtails in the flour
   seasoned with salt and pepper.
Heat the lard in a large flameproof
casserole and brown the oxtail
pieces, a few at a time. Remove
from the casserole.

2 Fry the onions in the casserole
   for 5 minutes until lightly
browned. Stir in any remaining
flour, the stock, wine, tomato
purée, lemon rind, bay leaves and
season well. Bring to the boil and
replace the meat.

3 Cover the pan with a tight-
   fitting lid and simmer the contents for 2 hours; skim well to
remove any excess fat.

4 Stir the carrots and parsnips
   into the casserole. Cover and
simmer for a further 2 hours or
until the meat is tender.

5 Skim all fat off the surface of
   the casserole, adjust the
seasoning and garnish with
chopped parsley.

Menu Suggestion
Braised oxtail is a rich, satisfying
dish for a midweek meal in winter.
Serve with plain boiled or mashed
potatoes and crisply cooked
winter cabbage.

BRAISED OXTAIL
Oxtail is an inexpensive cut of
beef with an excellent 'meaty'
flavour and wonderfully succulent texture if cooked slowly as
in this recipe. The main problem
with oxtail, however, is its fatti-
ness, which many people find off-
putting, and yet there is a simple
solution. Cook the casserole the
day before required and leave it
until completely cold. Chill it in
the refrigerator overnight, at the
end of which time the fat will
have risen to the surface and
formed a solid layer. Simply lift
off this layer and you will find a
thick, gelatinous gravy under-
neath, which becomes rich and
flavoursome on reheating.

STUFFED HEARTS

| 2.40 | £ | 363 cals |

Serves 8

8 lamb's hearts, each weighing about 175 g (6 oz)

50 g (2 oz) butter or margarine

1 small onion, skinned and chopped

100 g (4 oz) fresh breadcrumbs

10 ml (2 tsp) grated lemon rind

30 ml (2 tbsp) chopped fresh sage

salt and freshly ground pepper

pinch of grated nutmeg

1 egg, beaten

60 ml (4 tbsp) plain flour

30 ml (2 tbsp) vegetable oil

300 ml (½ pint) chicken stock

chopped fresh sage and grated lemon rind, to garnish

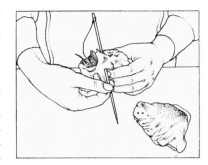

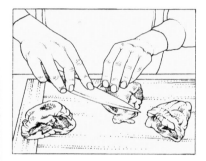

1 Wash the hearts thoroughly under cold running water. Trim them and remove any ducts.

2 Melt 25 g (1 oz) of the fat in a frying pan and lightly fry the onion for about 5 minutes until softened. Remove from the heat and stir in the breadcrumbs, lemon rind, parsley and seasonings. Bind with egg and mix well.

3 Fill the hearts with the stuffing and sew up neatly. Coat the hearts in the flour.

4 Heat the remaining fat and the oil in a flameproof casserole and brown the hearts well. Pour over the stock, season well and bring to the boil.

5 Cover and cook in the oven at 150°C (300°F) mark 2 for about 2 hours or until tender. Serve the hearts whole or sliced and pour the skimmed juices over. Garnish with sage and grated lemon rind.

Menu Suggestion
Serve with creamed potatoes and a dish of braised red cabbage, onion and apple, which can be cooked in the oven at the same time as the stuffed hearts.

STUFFED HEARTS

Hearts are inexpensive to buy, yet ideal for casseroling. Their dense, muscular tissue benefits from long, slow cooking, resulting in tender, moist meat which is amazingly lean. Lamb's hearts are the best size for stuffing, because one heart is just about the right quantity for one serving. Calf's and pig's hearts are larger, serving two to three; ox heart is larger still, and so tough that it is best chopped or thinly sliced rather than stuffed.

TRIPES À LA MODE DE CAEN
(TRIPE WITH CIDER AND CALVADOS)

6.15* | 351 cals

* may be cooked the day before and reheated (see step 4)

Serves 6

1 kg (2¼ lb) dressed tripe

1–2 pig's trotters

salt and freshly ground pepper

2 bay leaves

2 parsley sprigs

4 large onions, skinned

4 whole cloves

4 leeks, trimmed and sliced

2 carrots, peeled and sliced

3 celery sticks, trimmed and sliced

600 ml (1 pint) cider or dry white wine

60 ml (4 tbsp) Calvados

chopped fresh parsley, to garnish

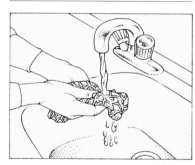

1 Wash the tripe very thoroughly. Blanch in boiling water for 5 minutes, then drain and rinse in cold running water.

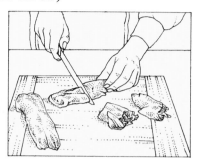

2 Divide up the trotters. Place in a casserole with the tripe, seasoning, herbs, onions (each stuck with a clove), leeks, carrots and celery. Add the cider or wine and the Calvados.

3 Cover and cook in the oven at 150°C (300°F) mark 2 for 6 hours until tender.

4 This dish may be left overnight. Remove the fat from the surface and take out the trotter bones and the herbs before reheating for serving. Garnish with chopped parsley.

Menu Suggestion

Tripes à la Mode de Caen is a very rich dish, which needs no accompaniment other than French bread. To refresh the palate, follow with a crisp, green salad tossed in a vinaigrette dressing.

TRIPES À LA MODE DE CAEN

This recipe for tripe (the bleached and partly boiled stomach lining of a cow) comes from Normandy in north-western France. This part of France has a reputation for its excellent cattle, and tripe is one of the local specialities—wedges of cold tripe which have been cooked 'à la mode de Caen' are a common sight in charcuteries in Normandy. The cider and Calvados in the recipe are also specialities of the region, where orchards of cider-apple trees can be seen almost everywhere. Normandy cider, called 'cidre bouche', is left to ferment naturally in the bottle, and is deceptively strong. Calvados is a kind of apple brandy, distilled from cider; it too is very strong—almost fiery in some cases. If French cider and Calvados prove difficult to obtain, use an ordinary dry cider and brandy instead.

KIDNEYS AND MUSHROOMS IN RED WINE

0.30	294–392 cals

Serves 3–4

50 g (2 oz) butter

2 onions, skinned and chopped

10 lamb's kidneys

45 ml (3 tbsp) plain flour

150 ml ($\frac{1}{4}$ pint) red wine

150 ml ($\frac{1}{4}$ pint) beef stock

bouquet garni

30 ml (2 tbsp) tomato purée

salt and freshly ground pepper

100 g (4 oz) mushrooms, sliced

chopped fresh parsley, to garnish

1 Melt the butter in a saucepan or a frying pan and fry the onions for about 5 minutes until golden brown.

2 Wash, skin and core the kidneys and cut them into halves lengthways. Add to the pan and cook for 5 minutes, stirring occasionally.

3 Stir in the flour, pour in the wine and stock and bring slowly to the boil. Stir in the bouquet garni, tomato purée, seasoning and mushrooms. Cover and simmer for about 15 minutes until the kidneys are tender.

4 Remove the bouquet garni and adjust the seasoning. Serve sprinkled with chopped parsley.

Menu Suggestion
Serve for an informal supper party with boiled long-grain rice and a mixed salad tossed in plenty of vinaigrette dressing.

SAUSAGE AND BEAN RAGOUT

2.30* £ ✳ 710 cals

* plus overnight soaking

Serves 4

125 g (4 oz) haricot beans, soaked overnight
125 g (4 oz) red kidney beans, soaked overnight
30 ml (2 tbsp) vegetable oil
450 g (1 lb) pork sausages
175 g (6 oz) onions, skinned and sliced
227 g (8 oz) can tomatoes
15 ml (1 tbsp) cornflour
15 ml (1 tbsp) chilli seasoning
30 ml (2 tbsp) tomato purée
350 ml (12 fl oz) dry cider
salt and freshly ground pepper

1 Drain the haricot and kidney beans and place in a saucepan. Cover with cold water, bring to the boil and boil rapidly for 10 minutes, then drain again.

2 Heat the oil in a large flame-proof casserole and fry the sausages for about 5 minutes until browned. Remove from the casserole and cut each sausage in half crossways.

3 Add the onions to the casserole and fry for 5 minutes until golden brown. Return the sausages to the casserole together with the beans and tomatoes.

4 Blend the cornflour, chilli seasoning and tomato purée with a little cider until smooth, then stir in the rest of the cider. Pour into the casserole, mix well and add pepper to taste.

5 Cover tightly and cook in the oven at 170°C (325°F) mark 3 for about 2 hours or until beans are tender. Add salt before serving the ragout.

Menu Suggestion
A filling midweek family meal, Sausage and Bean Ragout may be served with fresh French bread, boiled rice or creamed potatoes. Follow with a green salad and fresh fruit to complete the meal.

SALSICCIE CON PEPERONI
(ITALIAN SAUSAGE AND SWEET PEPPER CASSEROLE)

0.45	510 cals

Serves 4

450 g (1 lb) Italian frying sausages (*salsiccia*)

45 ml (3 tbsp) olive oil

25 g (1 oz) butter

1 large onion, skinned and chopped

3 peppers (1 green, 1 red, 1 yellow), cored, seeded and sliced

225 g (8 oz) can tomatoes

90 ml (6 tbsp) chicken or beef stock

60 ml (4 tbsp) dry white wine or water

5 ml (1 tsp) dried sage

5 ml (1 tsp) dried rosemary

salt and freshly ground pepper

chopped fresh parsley, to garnish

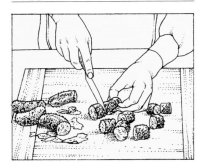

1 Plunge the sausages into a large pan of boiling water and simmer for 10 minutes. Drain, leave until cool enough to handle, then remove the skin and cut the sausages into bite-sized pieces.

2 Heat the oil with the butter in a flameproof casserole, add the onion and fry gently for 5 minutes until soft but not coloured.

3 Add the sausage and peppers and fry for a further 5 minutes, stirring constantly.

4 Mash the tomatoes with their juice in a bowl, then add to the casserole with the stock and wine. Bring slowly to boiling point, then lower the heat, add the herbs and seasoning to taste and simmer uncovered for 10–15 minutes. Taste and adjust seasoning, then garnish with parsley before serving.

Menu Suggestion
Serve this colourful Italian dish with risotto for an informal supper party. A salad of fennel and cucumber tossed in a minty olive oil and lemon juice dressing may be served afterwards to complete the meal.

SALSICCIE CON PEPERONI

Italian frying sausage sold in specialist delicatessens is available as individual sausages, usually called *salamelle*, or in one long piece called *luganega* or *salsiccia a metro*, which is cut and sold by the kg (lb). Both types are suitable for this recipe, but check with the shopkeeper before buying as some varieties are peppery hot and may not be to your taste. Italians eat a lot of this kind of sausage, which they either fry or grill, or sometimes boil. It is also used frequently in stuffings, and you may like to use it in recipes calling for sausagemeat — with its tasty herbs and spices, it is far less bland than most traditional pork or beef sausagemeats.

Poultry and Game

Poultry is always immensely popular no matter how it is cooked, but you will notice that casseroling lends moistness and flavour to these lean, tender meats which otherwise tend to be dry and sometimes bland. The recipes in this chapter give the flavour of poultry a real lift by combining the meat with strong-flavoured ingredients such as herbs, spices and fruits. Casseroling is also the perfect cooking method for older game birds, which can be tough and dry if cooked by fast or dry methods.

CHICKEN WITH GARLIC

| 2.15 | 208 cals |

Serves 6

60 ml (4 tbsp) olive or corn oil

1.8 kg (4 lb) chicken

1 sprig each of rosemary, thyme, savory and basil or 2.5 ml ($\frac{1}{2}$ tsp) dried

1 bay leaf

40 garlic cloves

salt and freshly ground pepper

grated nutmeg

300 ml ($\frac{1}{2}$ pint) hot water

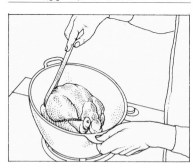

1 Heat the oil in a flameproof casserole and fry the chicken for about 8 minutes until browned on all sides. Remove chicken from the casserole.

2 Place the herbs in the base of the casserole. Arrange the garlic, unpeeled, in one layer over them. Place the chicken on top and season well with salt, pepper and nutmeg.

3 Cover and cook over a very low heat for $1\frac{1}{4}$–$1\frac{3}{4}$ hours until tender, adding a little hot water if necessary.

4 When cooked, remove the chicken and place on a warmed serving dish. Set aside and keep hot until required.

5 Strain the sauce into a bowl, pushing the garlic cloves through the sieve, using the back of a wooden spoon.

6 Add the hot water to the casserole and stir to lift the sediment. Return the sauce, taste and adjust seasoning, and simmer for 2 minutes or until hot. Transfer to a warm sauceboat and serve with the chicken.

Menu Suggestion
This French main course dish is traditionally served with rounds of French bread. A crisp green salad is usually served afterwards, to refresh the palate.

CHICKEN WITH GARLIC

In France, Poulet aux Quarantes Gousses d'Ail, is a popular recipe, and it's surprising how such a large number of garlic cloves tastes so mild. Any garlic residue can be used in the classic French potato dish Gratin Dauphinois, or another favourite French way of serving it is to spread it on slices of toasted baguette (French stick). This garlic-spread bread is then offered as an accompaniment to the chicken dish, and is considered a great delicacy by the French.

COQ AU VIN BLANC
(CHICKEN IN WHITE WINE)

| 1.45 | £ £ ✳* | 621–829 cals |

* freeze after step 7

Serves 6–8

175 g (6 oz) lean bacon, rinded and diced

75 g (3 oz) butter

450 g (1 lb) button onions, skinned

225 g (8 oz) button mushrooms

2.7 kg (6 lb) roasting chicken, jointed into 8 pieces

75 g (3 oz) plain flour

salt and freshly ground pepper

vegetable oil for frying

60 ml (4 tbsp) brandy

600 ml (1 pint) dry white wine

chicken stock

1 garlic clove, skinned and crushed

sprigs of fresh thyme or 2.5 ml ($\frac{1}{2}$ tsp) dried

2 bay leaves

6–8 pieces of French bread, in 1 cm ($\frac{1}{2}$ inch) slices, or 3 slices of white bread, crusts removed

chopped fresh parsley, to garnish

1 Blanch the bacon by dropping it into boiling water for 30 seconds. Lift out and dry on absorbent kitchen paper.

2 Melt 25 g (1 oz) of the butter in a large frying pan until foaming. Add the bacon and fry gently for 1 minute. Add the onions, increase the heat and fry until evenly browned. Lastly, add the mushrooms and fry for 2 minutes. Transfer the bacon and vegetables to a plate with a slotted spoon.

3 Coat the chicken joints with 50 g (2 oz) of the flour, seasoned with salt and pepper. Heat another 25 g (1 oz) butter and 30 ml (2 tbsp) oil in the frying pan, add the chicken, and fry until browned all over. Transfer the bacon, vegetables and chicken to an overproof casserole.

4 Warm the brandy, ignite and pour it over the chicken joints. Let the flames die down.

5 Pour 150 ml ($\frac{1}{4}$ pint) of the white wine into the frying pan. Bring to the boil, scraping any sediment from the bottom of the pan, then pour over the chicken joints in the casserole.

6 Add the bacon and vegetables to the casserole with the remaining wine and enough chicken stock to cover the joints. Add the garlic, herbs and seasoning to taste.

7 Bring to the boil, then cover and cook in the oven at 170°C (325°F) mark 3 for 1 hour, or until chicken is tender.

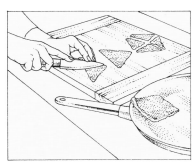

8 Meanwhile, fry the French bread or bread slices on each side in oil until golden brown. Drain well on absorbent kitchen paper. Cut each bread slice into triangles.

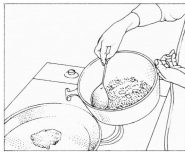

9 When cooked, remove the chicken and vegetables from the liquid, arrange on a serving dish, cover and keep warm. Skim the fat from the cooking liquid, then bring it to the boil.

11 Garnish with the French bread croûtes or white bread triangles and lots of chopped parsley.

10 Knead the remaining butter and remaining flour to a smooth paste (beurre manié). Add to the liquid in small amounts and bring to the boil, whisking all the time. Simmer for 2 minutes until thickened. Taste and adjust the seasoning.

Menu Suggestion
A classic French dish, Coq au Vin is traditionally served with steamed or boiled potatoes tossed in melted butter and finely chopped fresh parsley. A green vegetable such as petits pois, courgettes or mange-touts is also sometimes served.

COQ AU VIN BLANC
Coq au Vin Blanc—Chicken in White Wine—is simply a variation of the classic French dish Coq au Vin Rouge—Chicken in Red Wine. To be sure of the success of this dish, which makes an excellent dinner party main course, buy a good-quality French wine. It is a mistake to think that any inferior wine can be used for cooking, and any wine that is labelled 'cooking wine' should be treated with suspicion. Muscadet, Sancerre, Graves or white Burgundy are all suitable for this dish.

SPANISH CHICKEN

| 1.15 | ✳ | 513 cals |

Serves 4

| 60 ml (4 tbsp) olive oil |
| 1 onion, skinned and chopped |
| 2 garlic cloves, skinned and crushed |
| 4 chicken portions |
| 60 ml (4 tbsp) brandy |
| 2 small peppers (1 red and 1 green or yellow), cored, seeded and sliced |
| 4 large tomatoes, skinned and chopped |
| 150 ml (¼ pint) dry white wine |
| 150 ml (¼ pint) chicken stock or water |
| 10 ml (2 tsp) chopped fresh rosemary or 5 ml (1 tsp) dried |
| salt and freshly ground pepper |

1 Heat the oil in a flameproof casserole, add the onion and garlic and fry gently for 5 minutes until soft but not coloured.

2 Add the chicken portions and fry for a few minutes more, turning the chicken constantly so that the pieces become browned on all sides.

3 Warm the brandy gently in a small pan or ladle. Remove the casserole from the heat, pour the brandy over the chicken and set it alight with a match.

4 When the flames have died down, return the casserole to the heat and add the peppers and tomatoes. Fry over moderate heat for about 10 minutes, mashing the tomatoes down to a purée with a wooden spoon.

5 Pour in the wine and stock and bring slowly to boiling point. Lower the heat, add the rosemary and seasoning to taste, then cover and simmer for 30 minutes or until the chicken is tender when pierced with a skewer. Taste and adjust seasoning before serving.

Menu Suggestion

A quick-to-make main course for an informal dinner party, Spanish Chicken is best served with saffron rice or hot herb bread. Follow with a salad of shredded lettuce and finely chopped onion tossed in olive oil, lemon juice and salt and freshly ground pepper.

SPANISH CHICKEN

Olive oil, onion, garlic, peppers and tomatoes are all ingredients which conjure up a vivid image of colourful Spanish cookery. Wine and spirits also play quite a large part in the cuisine of Spain, although this is less well known than with French cookery, for example.

Don't worry about the high alcohol content of this recipe, which combines both brandy and wine together—a popular

Spanish combination. The actual alcohol content is burnt off by the flaming of the brandy, and evaporated by the heating of the wine, as long as the cooking time is at least 20 minutes, which it is in the case of the recipe above. If the alcohol were not eliminated in this way, the flavour of the finished dish would be raw and harsh. In this recipe the alcohol gives body and richness to the sauce.

CHICKEN DHANSAK

| 1.15 | ✳ | 568 cals |

Serves 4

40 g (1½ oz) ghee or clarified butter

1 onion, skinned and chopped

2.5 cm (1 inch) piece fresh root ginger, skinned and crushed

1–2 garlic cloves, skinned and crushed

4 chicken portions

5 ml (1 tsp) ground coriander

2.5 ml (½ tsp) chilli powder

2.5 ml (½ tsp) ground turmeric

1.25 ml (¼ tsp) ground cinnamon

salt

225 g (8 oz) red lentils, rinsed and drained

juice of 1 lime or lemon

fresh lime slices and coriander leaves, to garnish

1 Melt the ghee or butter in a flameproof casserole, add the onion, ginger and garlic and fry gently for 5 minutes until soft but not coloured.

2 Add the chicken portions and spices and fry for a few minutes more, turning the chicken constantly so that the pieces become coloured on all sides.

3 Pour enough water into the casserole to just cover the chicken. Add salt to taste, then the red lentils.

4 Bring slowly to boiling point, stirring, then lower the heat and cover the casserole. Simmer for 40 minutes or until the chicken is tender when pierced with a skewer. During cooking, turn the chicken in the sauce occasionally, and check that the lentils have not absorbed all the water and become too dry—add water if necessary.

5 Remove the chicken from the casserole and leave until cool enough to handle. Take the meat off the bones, discarding the skin. Cut the meat into bite-sized pieces, return to the casserole and heat through thoroughly. Stir in the lime or lemon juice; taste and add more salt if necessary. Garnish with fresh lime slices and coriander leaves before serving.

Menu Suggestion

Serve this hot Indian curry with boiled or fried basmati rice and a yogurt and cucumber salad (raita) for a cooling effect. Indian bread such as paratha or puri (packet mixes are now widely available) can also be served as an appetising accompaniment.

CHICKEN DHANSAK

Ghee or clarified butter is used frequently in Asian cookery. To make it, simmer melted butter in a heavy pan until a thick froth forms on top. Lower the heat and continue simmering until froth starts to separate and sediment settles at the bottom. Cool slightly, then strain through a metal sieve lined with muslin or a clean tea-towel. Discard sediment. Store ghee in refrigerator.

CARIBBEAN CHICKEN

0.50*	447 cals

* plus overnight marinating

Serves 4

4 boneless chicken breasts, skinned

15 ml (1 tbsp) vinegar

425 g (15 oz) can pineapple slices in natural juice

10 ml (2 tsp) soft brown sugar

salt and freshly ground pepper

45 ml (3 tbsp) vegetable oil

175 g (6 oz) long grain rice

1½ green, red or yellow peppers, cored, seeded and sliced

Tabasco sauce, to taste

60 ml (4 tbsp) dark rum

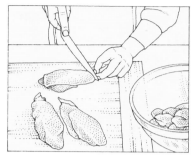

1 Cut the chicken into bite-sized pieces and place in a bowl. Make the marinade. Mix together the vinegar, pineapple juice, sugar, 10 ml (2 tsp) salt and pepper to taste. Pour over the chicken, cover and leave to marinate overnight. Turn the chicken in the marinade occasionally during this time.

2 Drain the chicken and reserve the marinade. Make the marinade up to 600 ml (1 pint) with water and set aside.

3 Heat the oil in a flameproof casserole, add the chicken and fry over moderate heat until turning colour on all sides. Add the rice and most of the pepper and fry for 5 minutes, stirring.

4 Pour in the marinade and bring slowly to the boil. Stir once, then shake in Tabasco sauce to taste and lower the heat. Cover and simmer for 20 minutes or until the chicken and rice are tender and most of the liquid has been absorbed.

5 Chop the pineapple and add to the casserole with the rum. Fold in gently and heat through. Taste and adjust seasoning before serving. Garnish with remaining pepper slices.

Menu Suggestion

Caribbean Chicken combines meat, vegetables and rice in one dish. Serve with hot French bread and follow with a green salad, for an informal meal.

Stoved Chicken

| 2.15 | f | 586 cals |

Serves 4

50 g (2 oz) butter

1.4 kg (3 lb) chicken, jointed

100 g (4 oz) streaky bacon, rinded and chopped

1.1 kg (2½ lb) floury potatoes such as King Edwards

2 large onions, skinned and sliced

salt and freshly ground pepper

10 ml (2 tsp) chopped fresh thyme or 2.5 ml (½ tsp) dried

600 ml (1 pint) chicken stock

snipped chives, to garnish

1 Melt 25 g (1 oz) of the butter in a frying pan and fry the chicken and bacon for 5 minutes until lightly browned.

2 Peel the potatoes and cut into 5 mm (¼ inch) slices. Place a thick layer of potato slices, then sliced onion, in the base of a casserole. Season well, add the thyme and dot with butter.

3 Add the chicken, season and dot with butter. Cover with the remaining onions and finally a layer of potatoes. Season and dot with butter. Pour over the stock.

4 Cover and cook in the oven at 150°C (300°F) mark 2 for about 2 hours until the chicken is tender and the potatoes are cooked, adding a little more hot stock if necessary.

5 Just before serving sprinkle snipped chives over the top of the dish.

Menu Suggestion

Chicken and potatoes are cooked together in this casserole recipe. A seasonal vegetable such as carrots, peas or green beans is all that is needed for a family meal.

STOVED CHICKEN

This hearty dish made with simple, everyday ingredients would originally have been made with a boiling fowl, but nowadays these are not so easy to obtain, so an oven-ready or roasting chicken is used instead. The recipe originated in Scotland, where it is also sometimes called 'stovies', from the French verb 'étouffer', meaning to cook in an enclosed pot. During the alliance between the Scottish and the French in the 17th century, there were many words such as this one with a French derivation. Stoved Chicken or Stovies used to be served at rural weddings in the Highlands, but this custom has died out now and the dish has become traditional family fare.

HINDLE WAKES

3.15*	£	281–421 cals

* plus overnight soaking

Serves 4–6

1.6 kg (3½ lb) boiling chicken with giblets, trussed

600 ml (1 pint) water

salt and freshly ground pepper

50 g (2 oz) butter or margarine

450 g (1 lb) leeks, sliced and washed

6 carrots, peeled and thickly sliced

225 g (8 oz) prunes, soaked overnight and stoned

25 g (1 oz) plain flour

1 Place the giblets in a saucepan with the water and 5 ml (1 tsp) salt. Bring to the boil, then cover and simmer for 30 minutes.

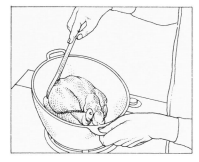

2 Meanwhile, melt 25 g (1 oz) of the fat in a large flame-proof casserole and fry the chicken for about 8 minutes until browned all over. Remove from casserole.

3 Fry the leeks and carrots for 3 minutes. Return the chicken and add the drained prunes. Strain in the giblet stock and season with pepper.

4 Cover and cook in the oven at 170°C (325°F) mark 3 for about 2–2½ hours or until tender.

5 Arrange the chicken, vege-tables and prunes on a large warmed platter. Keep hot.

6 Skim any fat off the sauce. Blend together the remaining fat and the flour to form a paste. Add to the sauce, a little at a time, and stir over a gentle heat until thickened. Do not boil. Adjust the seasoning to taste and serve the sauce separately.

Menu Suggestion
Serve this old English dish with jacket baked potatoes or creamed potatoes and a green vegetable.

TURKEY PAPRIKA WITH PASTA

| 0.40 | 385 cals |

Serves 4

30 ml (2 tbsp) vegetable oil

75 g (3 oz) onion, skinned and sliced

450 g (1 lb) turkey breasts

10 ml (2 tsp) paprika

450 ml ($\frac{3}{4}$ pint) chicken stock

salt and freshly ground pepper

1 green pepper, cored, seeded and sliced

100 g (4 oz) small pasta shapes

142 ml (5 fl oz) soured cream

paprika, to garnish

1 Heat the oil in a large sauté pan and fry the onion for 5 minutes until golden brown.

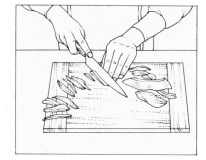

2 Skin the turkey breasts, discard any bone and cut flesh into small finger-sized pieces.

3 Add the turkey and paprika to the pan and toss over a moderate heat for 2 minutes.

4 Stir in the stock and seasoning and bring to the boil. Add the green pepper and pasta, cover and simmer gently for 15–20 minutes until turkey and pasta are tender.

5 Stir in the soured cream and adjust the seasoning. To serve, garnish with a little paprika.

Menu Suggestion
Quick and easy to make, this casserole needs no accompaniment other than a crisp green salad.

TURKEY GROUNDNUT STEW

| 1.15 | 465–698 cals |

Serves 4–6

30 ml (2 tbsp) vegetable oil

2 onions, skinned and chopped

1 garlic clove, skinned and crushed

1 large green pepper, cored, seeded and chopped

900 g (2 lb) boneless turkey, cut into cubes

175 g (6 oz) shelled peanuts

600 ml (1 pint) chicken stock

salt and freshly ground pepper

60 ml (4 tbsp) crunchy peanut butter

10 ml (2 tsp) tomato purée

225 g (8 oz) tomatoes, skinned and roughly chopped

2.5–5 ml ($\frac{1}{2}$–1 tsp) cayenne pepper

few drops of Tabasco sauce

chopped green pepper, to garnish

1 Heat the oil in a flameproof casserole, add the onion, garlic and green pepper and fry gently for 5 minutes until they are soft but not coloured.

2 Add the turkey and fry for a few minutes more, turning constantly until well browned on all sides.

3 Add the peanuts, stock and salt and pepper to taste and bring slowly to boiling point. Lower the heat, cover and simmer for 45 minutes or until the turkey is tender.

4 Remove the turkey from the cooking liquid with a slotted spoon and set aside. Leave the cooking liquid to cool for about 5 minutes.

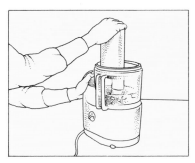

5 Work the cooking liquid and nuts in an electric blender or food processor, half at a time, until quite smooth. Return to the pan with the remaining ingredients, add the turkey and reheat. Taste and adjust seasoning before serving, adding more cayenne if a hot flavour is liked. Garnish with chopped green pepper.

Menu Suggestion

Groundnut stews are traditionally served in the Caribbean with plain boiled rice and a dish of root vegetables such as turnip, swede or parsnip. If liked, hot pepper sauce can also be offered as an additional accompaniment.

TURKEY GROUNDNUT STEW

Groundnut stews originated in West Africa, where groundnuts (or peanuts as we call them) grow in profusion. The cook would buy fresh peanut paste from the market to make groundnut stew, which was a popular Sunday lunch dish — served with ice-cold beer and garnished with fried bananas. Due to the slave trade, groundnut stews spread to the West Indies, becoming an integral part of the local cuisine.

Recipes for groundnut stew vary enormously, some using beef, others chicken, turkey or rabbit. Some recipes use only peanut butter, others like this one, a combination of whole peanuts and peanut butter, which is more authentic. If you like, you can toast or roast the peanuts after shelling, for a darker colour.

JUGGED HARE

| 3.30 | £ £ ✳ | 469 cals |

Serves 6

1.6 kg (3½ lb) hare, jointed, with
  its blood

75 ml (5 tbsp) seasoned plain flour

5 ml (1 tsp) red wine vinegar

125 g (4 oz) streaky bacon, rinded
  and chopped

50 g (2 oz) butter

900 ml (1½ pints) beef stock

150 ml (¼ pint) port

5 ml (1 tsp) dried marjoram

45 ml (3 tbsp) redcurrant jelly

2 onions, skinned

12 whole cloves

salt and freshly ground pepper

parsley sprigs, to garnish

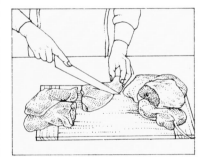

1 Wipe the hare and divide into smaller pieces if necessary. Toss in the seasoned flour.

2 Mix the blood with the vinegar (to keep it fresh), cover and refrigerate until required.

3 Meanwhile, fry the bacon in its own fat in a large flame-proof casserole for about 5 minutes until browned. Remove from the pan. Add the butter to the pan and fry the hare joints for 5 minutes until they are lightly browned.

4 Add the stock, port, marjoram and redcurrant jelly with the onions studded with the cloves. Replace bacon and season well.

5 Bring to the boil, cover and cook in the oven at 170°C (325°F) mark 3 for 3 hours until tender. Remove hare to a serving dish and keep warm. Discard the onions.

6 Mix the blood with some cooking juices until smooth. Add to the pan and heat. Adjust seasoning and pour over hare. Garnish with parsley sprigs.

Menu Suggestion
Serve Jugged Hare with dumplings (see page 157).

OLD ENGLISH GAME STEW

3.00	✳*	542 cals

* freeze after step 4

Serves 6

225 g (8 oz) chuck steak

700 g (1½ lb) stewing venison

75 g (3 oz) butter

4 large celery sticks, trimmed and roughly sliced

2 onions, skinned and finely sliced

45 ml (3 tbsp) plain flour

150 ml (¼ pint) port

450 ml (¾ pint) chicken stock

salt and freshly ground pepper

100 g (4 oz) streaky bacon

1 small onion, skinned and finely chopped

125 g (4 oz) fresh white breadcrumbs

1.25 ml (¼ tsp) dried thyme

1 egg, beaten

celery leaves, to garnish

1 Cut the steak and venison into cubes 2.5 cm (1 inch) square, discarding excess fat and sinew.

2 Melt 50 g (2 oz) of the butter in a large flameproof casserole and fry the steak pieces for about 5 minutes until browned. Remove from the pan and drain. Add the venison to the pan and fry for about 8 minutes until browned. Remove from the pan.

3 Add the celery and sliced onions to the pan and lightly brown for about 5 minutes. Stir in the flour, port, stock and seasoning and bring to the boil.

4 Return the steak and venison to the casserole. Cover tightly and cook in the oven at 180°C (350°F) mark 4 for 1½–2 hours or until the meats are almost tender.

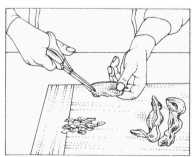

5 Meanwhile make the forcemeat balls. Grill the bacon until crisp and, removing rind, snip into small pieces.

6 Melt the remaining butter in a saucepan and fry the chopped onion for about 5 minutes until golden. Stir into the breadcrumbs together with the bacon, thyme and seasoning.

7 Bind the mixture with beaten egg and shape into 6 even-sized balls.

8 Place them between the meat in the casserole and cover. Increase the oven temperature to 190°C (375°F) mark 5 and return the casserole to the bottom of the oven for a further 30 minutes. Adjust the seasoning and garnish with celery leaves.

Menu Suggestion

Serve this rich stew for a winter dinner party with creamed or jacket baked potatoes and a selection of seasonal vegetables.

RABBIT CASSEROLE WITH CIDER AND MUSTARD

| 2.30 | 445 cals |

Serves 4

50 g (2 oz) butter or margarine

100 g (4 oz) streaky bacon, rinded and diced

12–18 small button onions, skinned

1 rabbit, jointed

25 g (1 oz) plain flour

salt and freshly ground pepper

10 ml (2 tsp) French mustard

300 ml ($\frac{1}{2}$ pint) dry cider

450 ml ($\frac{3}{4}$ pint) chicken stock

1 Melt the fat in a frying pan and fry the bacon and onions for 5 minutes until lightly browned. Remove to a casserole with a slotted spoon.

2 Coat the rabbit in a little flour seasoned with salt and pepper and fry in the pan for about 8 minutes until golden brown. Arrange in the casserole.

3 Stir the remaining flour and the French mustard into the pan. Gradually add the cider and stock. Season, bring to the boil and pour over the rabbit.

4 Cover and cook in the oven at 170°C (325°F) mark 3 for about 2 hours or until the rabbit is tender. Adjust the seasoning before serving.

Menu Suggestion

A delicious main course dish for a winter dinner party, Rabbit Casserole with Cider and Mustard tastes good with ribbon noodles tossed in butter and chopped fresh parsley. Finish with a crisp green salad in a vinaigrette dressing.

PIGEON AND CABBAGE CASSEROLE

2.00	547 cals

Serves 4

1 green, white or red cabbage, quartered

salt and freshly ground pepper

25 g (1 oz) bacon fat or butter

2–4 pigeons, depending on size

8 chipolatas

2 onions, skinned and chopped

6 streaky bacon rashers, rinded and chopped

2.5 ml ($\frac{1}{2}$ tsp) ground cloves

300 ml ($\frac{1}{2}$ pint) red wine or wine and stock

1 Blanch the cabbage for 5 minutes in boiling salted water. Drain.

2 Melt the bacon fat or butter in a large frying pan and fry the pigeons and chipolatas for about 8 minutes until browned all over. Remove from the pan. Fry the onions in the fat remaining in the pan for 5 minutes until golden. Sprinkle the chopped bacon over the base of a casserole.

3 Shred the cabbage and mix with the onions and ground cloves. Spread half the cabbage mixture over the bacon, season with pepper and place the pigeons and chipolatas on top. Cover with the remaining cabbage, season with more pepper and pour over the wine.

4 Cover and cook in the oven at 170°C (325°F) mark 3 for about 1$\frac{1}{2}$ hours or until the birds are tender. Serve hot.

Menu Suggestion
Simple homely fare, this pigeon casserole is best served with mashed or creamed potatoes and a seasonal vegetable such as carrots or broccoli.

PIGEON AND CABBAGE CASSEROLE

For this recipe, an older pigeon can be used because of the long, slow cooking. Young pigeons and squabs (pigeons under 5 weeks old) are best reserved for roasting and grilling. Although classed as game birds, pigeons do not have a closed season and are therefore available all year round. Wood pigeons, which weigh around 700 g (1$\frac{1}{2}$ lb) each, are the ones to look for in your local poulterer or game dealer, especially in the spring and summer months, when they are said to be at their best. For those who find the flavour of game, rather strong, and their smell too 'high', pigeons are ideal. They are not hung like other game birds and are therefore quite mild in flavour, like poultry.

GUINEA FOWL WITH GRAPES

| 1.00 | 🍳 | £ £ | 449–545 cals |

Serves 4

350 g (12 oz) seedless white grapes

30 ml (2 tbsp) brandy

1 garlic clove, skinned and finely sliced

rosemary sprigs

salt and freshly ground pepper

2 prepared guinea fowl

4 streaky bacon rashers, rinded

50 g (2 oz) butter

200 ml (7 fl oz) dry white wine

watercress, to garnish

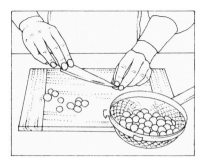

1 Blanch the grapes in boiling water for 2 minutes, then re-move skins with a sharp knife.

2 Put the grapes in a bowl. Spoon over the brandy and leave to marinate, turning from time to time.

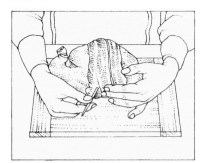

3 Put a few garlic slices, a sprig of rosemary and seasoning inside each bird. Wrap two bacon rashers round each one and secure with wooden cocktail sticks.

4 Place the guinea fowl in a casserole with the butter. Season and sprinkle with a little extra rosemary. Cover and cook in the oven at 220°C (425°F) mark 7 for 15 minutes.

5 Bring the wine to the boil in a pan. Turn the guinea fowl over and pour over the wine. Cook, uncovered, for a further 15 minutes until the birds are tender.

6 Remove the guinea fowl to a warmed serving dish and keep hot. Add the grapes to the sauce and heat through.

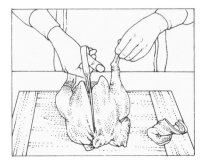

7 Remove the bacon and cut the guinea fowl in half with game scissors. Arrange the bacon over the halves, pour the sauce over and garnish with watercress.

Menu Suggestion
Serve with game chips or roast potatoes, brussels sprouts and redcurrant jelly.

NORMANDY PHEASANT

`1.30` 🝙 £ £ `588 cals`

Serves 4

1 large pheasant, jointed
salt and freshly ground pepper
25 g (1 oz) plain flour
60 ml (4 tbsp) vegetable oil
2 onions, skinned and sliced
2 celery sticks, trimmed and sliced
225 g (8 oz) cooking apples, peeled, cored and sliced
50 ml (2 tbsp) brandy or Calvados
150 ml (¼ pint) chicken stock
300 ml (½ pint) dry cider
1 bay leaf
2 eating apples, cored and sliced into 1 cm (½ inch) rings
15 g (½ oz) butter
2 egg yolks
150 ml (5 fl oz) single cream
fresh coriander sprigs, to garnish

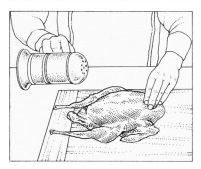

1 Coat the pheasant in seasoned flour. Heat the oil in a flame-proof casserole and fry the pheasant for 5 minutes until browned. Remove from casserole.

2 Fry the onions and celery in the casserole for 5 minutes. Add the apples and pheasant.

3 Heat, ignite and pour the brandy or Calvados over the pheasant. When flames have died add the stock, cider and bay leaf.

4 Bring to the boil, cover and cook in the oven at 180°C (350°F) mark 4 for about 1 hour. Put pheasant on a warmed platter.

5 Meanwhile, fry the apple rings in the butter until golden on both sides. Keep warm.

6 Beat the yolks into the cream and stir into the cooking juices. Warm through then pour over pheasant. Surround with the apple rings and garnish with chopped parsley.

Menu Suggestion
Serve with game chips or roast potatoes, red cabbage casserole and a seasonal green vegetable such as brussels sprouts or fresh broccoli.

Fish and Shellfish

Fish and shellfish are usually cooked quickly by grilling, frying and sautéeing, but this is no reason why they shouldn't also be used in casseroles. As long as they are not overcooked, fish and shellfish taste wonderfully moist and succulent in casseroles — and they are economical in that they have very little waste compared with meat. The rather bland flavours of some fish and shellfish lend themselves to rich and pungent sauces, and the recipes in this chapter illustrate this point perfectly.

LA BOURRIDE
(MEDITERRANEAN FISH STEW WITH AÏOLI)

| 1.00* | 🍳 | £ £ | 984 cals |

* plus extra time for making fish stock

Serves 4

1 egg yolk

10 garlic cloves, skinned

300 ml (½ pint) olive oil

juice of 1 lemon

5 ml (1 tsp) lukewarm water

salt and freshly ground pepper

900 g (2 lb) firm white fish fillets (e.g. bass, turbot, whiting, monkfish or halibut), skinned

1.1 litres (2 pints) homemade fish stock (see page 152)

1 small onion, skinned and thinly sliced

1 leek, trimmed and thinly sliced

1–2 parsley sprigs

1 bay leaf

1 thin strip of orange rind

1 small baguette (French stick), sliced, to serve

chopped fresh parsley, to garnish

1 First make the aïoli. Put the egg yolk and 8 roughly chopped garlic cloves in a mortar and crush with a pestle. Add the oil a drop at a time and work until ingredients emulsify and thicken.

2 Continue adding the oil in a thin, steady stream, beating vigorously until the mayonnaise is very thick and smooth.

3 Beat in the lemon juice and water, and salt and pepper to taste. Set aside in a cool place.

4 Cut the fish into thick chunks and place in a large saucepan. Pour in the stock, then add the next five ingredients, with the remaining garlic, halved, and salt and pepper to taste. Cover and simmer for 15 minutes until tender.

5 Transfer the fish and vegetables with a slotted spoon to a warmed serving dish. Keep warm.

6 Strain cooking liquid into a jug and blend a few spoonfuls into the aïoli. Toast the sliced baguette and keep warm.

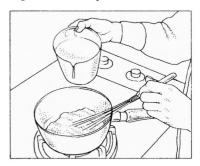

7 Put the aïoli in a heavy-based pan, then gradually whisk in the remaining cooking liquid. Heat through gently, stirring constantly. Adjust seasoning. Pour over the fish and sprinkle with parsley. Serve at once, with the toast.

Menu Suggestion
La Bourride needs no accompaniment other than the toasted baguette in the recipe.

SPANISH COD WITH PEPPERS, TOMATOES AND GARLIC

| 1.30 | ⏚ £ £ | 324 cals |

Serves 4

700 g (1½ lb) cod fillets

1.1 litres (1¾ pints) mussels or about 450 g (1 lb) weight

30 ml (2 tbsp) vegetable oil

2 onions, skinned and sliced

1 red pepper, cored, seeded and sliced

1 green pepper, cored, seeded and sliced

1–2 garlic cloves, skinned and crushed

450 g (1 lb) tomatoes, skinned and chopped

300 ml (½ pint) white wine

2.5 ml (½ tsp) Tabasco sauce

1 bay leaf

salt and freshly ground pepper

1 Using a sharp knife, skin the cod and cut it into chunks.

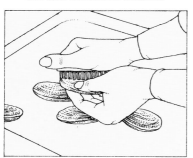

2 Scrub the mussels, discarding any which are open. Place in a pan, cover and cook over a high heat for about 8 minutes or until mussels have opened.

3 Shell all but four mussels. Heat the oil in a frying pan and cook the onions, peppers and garlic for about 5 minutes until starting to soften. Add the tomatoes and wine, bring to the boil and simmer for 5 minutes, then add the Tabasco.

4 Layer the fish and vegetables in a casserole and add the bay leaf and seasoning. Pour over the wine. Push the four mussels in shells into the top layer. Cover and cook in the oven at 180°C (350°F) mark 4 for 1 hour. Serve hot.

Menu Suggestion
Serve with hot French bread, followed by a crisp green salad tossed in an olive oil and lemon juice dressing.

SPANISH COD WITH PEPPERS, TOMATOES AND GARLIC

As soon as you get fresh mussels home from the fishmonger, immerse them in a bowl of cold water until you are ready to start dealing with them. If you add 15 ml (1 tbsp) oatmeal to the water, the live mussels will feed on it and this will help 'flush them out' so that you can be sure they are thoroughly clean inside. If the water becomes very murky during this time, replace it with fresh water and more oatmeal. Before preparation in step 2 of the recipe, tap any open mussels against the bowl or work surface—if they do not close they should be thrown away.

ITALIAN SQUID STEW

1.30* 🥂 🥂 320 cals

* plus 3 hours marinating

Serves 4

1 kg (2¼ lb) small squid

75 ml (5 tbsp) olive oil

salt and freshly ground pepper

75 ml (3 fl oz) dry white wine

2 garlic cloves, skinned and
   crushed

juice of ½ lemon

15 ml (1 tbsp) chopped fresh
   parsley

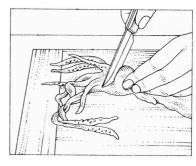

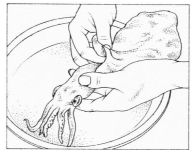

1 Wash the squid in plenty of cold water. Grip the head and tentacles firmly and pull them away from the body. The entrails will follow. Discard these and pull out transparent quill.

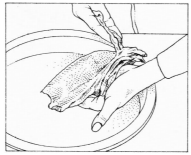

2 With your hands, carefully peel the skin from the body and the fins of the squid.

3 Cut the tentacles from head and remove the skin. Reserve two ink sacs being careful not to pierce them. Discard rest of head.

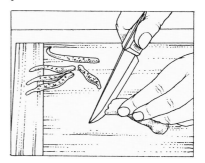

4 Cut the squid bodies into 0.5 cm (¼ inch) rings. Place in a bowl with the tentacles and spoon over 45 ml (3 tbsp) of the oil and season well. Leave for 3 hours.

5 Pour the squid and marinade into a large frying pan and cook the squid for 5 minutes, turning frequently. Add the wine and garlic and cook for a further 5 minutes. Add the ink sacs, breaking them up with a spoon.

6 Cover and cook over a low heat for about 40 minutes until the squid is tender.

7 Add the remaining oil, the lemon juice and parsley. Stir for 3 minutes over a high heat, adjust the seasoning and serve.

Menu Suggestion
In Italy, this rich stew of squid in white wine would be served with plain boiled rice or toasted bread.

CREAMY FISH CASSEROLE

1.30	379–569 cals

Serves 4–6

700 g (1½ lb) cod steaks, skinned and
   cut into bite-sized pieces
30 ml (2 tbsp) plain flour
salt and freshly ground pepper
40 g (1½ oz) butter
15 ml (1 tbsp) vegetable oil
600 ml (1 pint) dry cider
2 bay leaves, crumbled
900 g (2 lb) old floury potatoes,
   scrubbed
150 ml (5 fl oz) single cream
30 ml (2 tbsp) chopped fresh
   parsley

1 Coat the pieces of cod in the flour seasoned with salt and pepper to taste.

2 Melt 25 g (1 oz) of the butter with the oil in a frying pan, add the pieces of cod and fry gently until golden on all sides. Remove from the pan with a slotted spoon and set aside.

3 Pour the cider into the frying pan and stir to dislodge the sediment from the bottom and sides of the pan. Add the bay leaves and salt and pepper to taste. Bring to the boil and simmer for a few minutes, then pour into a jug.

4 Blanch the potatoes in their skins in boiling salted water for 10 minutes. Drain, leave until cool enough to handle, then peel off the skins and slice.

5 Put half the fish in the bottom of a shallow casserole. Stir the cream into the cider mixture, then pour half over the fish.

6 Cover with half the potato slices, overlapping them so that they cover the fish completely. Sprinkle with half the parsley. Put the remaining fish on top of the potatoes, then pour over the remaining cider and cream.

7 Cover with the remaining potato slices as before, then dot with the remaining butter. Cook in the oven at 190°C (375°F) mark 5 for 45 minutes. Sprinkle the remaining parsley over the top before serving.

Menu Suggestion
Serve for a family supper accompanied by a seasonal green vegetable such as courgettes or French beans. Ice-cold dry cider is the ideal drink with this casserole.

SMOKED HADDOCK WITH CREAM AND PERNOD

| 0.40 | £ £ | 382 cals |

Serves 4

4 smoked haddock fillets, about
   700 g (1½ lb) total weight
300 ml (½ pint) milk
few slices of onion
2 bay leaves
few black peppercorns
2.5 ml (½ tsp) crushed fennel seeds
150 ml (5 fl oz) double cream
15 g (½ oz) butter
60 ml (4 tbsp) Pernod
salt and freshly ground pepper
fennel sprigs, to garnish

1 Put the smoked haddock fillets in a large flameproof casserole. Pour in the milk and add the onion slices, bay leaves, peppercorns and fennel seeds. Pour in a little water if the liquid does not completely cover the smoked haddock.

2 Bring slowly to boiling point, then lower the heat, cover and simmer gently for 15 minutes or until the fish flakes easily when tested with a fork.

3 Remove the fish fillets from the cooking liquid and then flake into chunky pieces. Discard all skin and any bones.

4 Strain the cooking liquid and return to the rinsed-out pan. Boil to reduce slightly, then add the cream, butter and Pernod and boil again until the sauce thickens.

5 Return the fish to the liquid and heat through. Add salt and pepper to taste (taking care not to add too much salt as the fish is salty), then transfer to a warmed serving dish. Garnish with fennel sprigs and serve immediately.

Menu Suggestion
A rich and filling dinner party main course, best served with a plain accompaniment such as boiled rice or duchesse potatoes. If liked, the quantities may be halved and the dish served as a first course, with hot French bread.

SMOKED HADDOCK WITH CREAM AND PERNOD

As a starter this dish is most unusual, with its subtle flavouring of fennel and aniseed. Serve it for a special dinner party when you want to surprise your guests with something just that little bit different, but be sure to serve something quite plain as the main course.

   The choice of smoked haddock at the fishmonger can sometimes be confusing. The bright yellow fish sold as 'golden cutlets' is in fact smoked cod. Thicker than smoked haddock, it is an excellent fish for dishes like this one where the fish needs to be flaked into chunky pieces.

INDONESIAN FISH CURRY

| 0.40 | 287 cals |

Serves 4

1 small onion, skinned and chopped

1 garlic clove, skinned and chopped

2.5 cm (1 inch) piece fresh root ginger, skinned and chopped

5 ml (1 tsp) ground turmeric

2.5 ml ($\frac{1}{2}$ tsp) laos powder (see box)

1.25 ml ($\frac{1}{4}$ tsp) chilli powder

30 ml (2 tbsp) vegetable oil

salt

700 g (1$\frac{1}{2}$ lb) haddock fillets, skinned and cut into bite-sized pieces

225 g (8 oz) peeled prawns

300 ml ($\frac{1}{2}$ pint) coconut milk (see box)

juice of 1 lime

shredded coconut and lime wedges, to garnish

1 Work the first seven ingredients in an electric blender or processor with 2.5 ml ($\frac{1}{2}$ tsp) salt.

2 Transfer the mixture to a flameproof casserole and fry gently, stirring, for 5 minutes. Add the haddock pieces and prawns and fry for a few minutes more, tossing fish to coat with the spice mixture.

3 Pour in the coconut milk, shake the pan and turn the fish gently in the liquid. (Take care not to break up the pieces of fish.) Bring slowly to boiling point, then lower the heat, cover and simmer for 10 minutes until tender.

4 Add the lime juice, taste and adjust seasoning, then transfer to a warmed serving dish and sprinkle with coconut. Serve hot, garnished with lime wedges.

Menu Suggestion
Serve with plain boiled rice, prawn crackers and lime pickle.

INDONESIAN FISH CURRY
Laos powder is used extensively in the cooking of Southeast Asia; it comes from a root rather like ginger and has a peppery hot taste. Look for it in specialist delicatessens in small bottles, sometimes labelled galangal or galingale. To make 300 ml ($\frac{1}{2}$ pint) coconut milk, break 100 g (4 oz) block creamed coconut into a measuring jug, pour in boiling hot water up to the 300 ml ($\frac{1}{2}$ pint) mark and stir to dissolve. Strain before using.

MONKFISH WITH LIME AND PRAWNS

| 0.45 | £ £ | 294 cals |

Serves 4

550 g (1¼ lb) monkfish
salt and freshly ground pepper
15 ml (1 tbsp) plain flour
30 ml (2 tbsp) vegetable oil
1 small onion, skinned and chopped
1 garlic clove, skinned and chopped
225 g (8 oz) tomatoes, skinned and chopped
150 ml (¼ pint) dry white wine
finely grated rind and juice of 1 lime
pinch of sugar
100 g (4 oz) peeled prawns
lime slices, to garnish

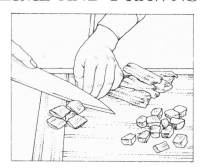

1 Using a sharp knife, skin the fish, if necessary, then cut fish into 5 cm (1 inch) chunks and toss in seasoned flour.

2 Heat the oil in a flameproof casserole and gently fry the onion and garlic for 5 minutes. Add fish and fry until golden.

3 Stir in the tomatoes, wine, rind and juice of the lime, sugar and seasoning. Bring to the boil.

4 Cover and cook in the oven at 180°C (350°F) mark 4 for 15 minutes. Add the prawns and continue to cook for a further 15 minutes until the monkfish is tender. Garnish with lime slices.

Menu Suggestion
Served in a ring of saffron rice, this Monkfish Casserole with Lime and Prawns makes an exceptionally pretty main course dish for a dinner party.

113

TROUT POACHED IN WINE

| 0.45 | £ £ | 357 cals |

Serves 4

4 small trout, with heads on
salt and freshly ground pepper
50 g (2 oz) butter
1 large onion, skinned and sliced
2 celery sticks, trimmed and
sliced
2 carrots, peeled and very thinly
sliced
300 ml (½ pint) dry white wine
bouquet garni
15 ml (1 tbsp) plain flour
lemon wedges and chopped fresh
parsley, to garnish

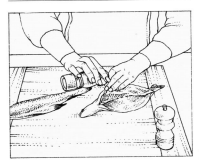

1 Wash the trout under cold running water and drain. Pat dry and season the insides.

2 Melt 25 g (1 oz) of the butter in a small saucepan, add the onion, celery and carrots and stir well to cover with butter. Cover and sweat for 5 minutes.

3 Lay the vegetables in a greased casserole and arrange the fish on top. Pour over the wine and add the bouquet garni.

4 Cover tightly and cook in the oven at 180°C (350°F) mark 4 for about 25 minutes until the trout are cooked.

5 Transfer the trout and vegetables to a warmed serving dish and keep hot.

6 Pour the cooking juices into a small pan, discarding the bouquet garni. Blend together the remaining butter and the flour. Whisk into the sauce and simmer gently, stirring, until thickened. Pour into a sauceboat or jug. Garnish the trout with lemon wedges and parsley.

Menu Suggestion
Serve with steamed or boiled new potatoes and a seasonal green vegetable or salad.

TROUT POACHED IN WINE

If you are unused to buying whole fresh fish at the fishmonger, you may find the different types of trout confusing. Sea trout are the larger of the species, so called because they have migrated to the sea from the rivers. Some fishmongers call them 'salmon trout', because their flesh is firm and salmony pink, and they can be used as an inexpensive alternative to fresh salmon.

For this recipe you will need to buy freshwater trout, i.e. river, rainbow or lake trout, which are now becoming increasingly widely available, both fresh and frozen, at supermarkets. Look for shiny, slippery skin and bright eyes—both good indications of freshness.

SWEDISH HERRINGS

1.00*	£	452 cals

* plus 2–3 hours cooling

Serves 4

4 fresh herrings, filleted

salt and freshly ground pepper

4 whole cloves

2 dried chillies

12 peppercorns

1 bay leaf

1 blade of mace

60 ml (4 tbsp) malt vinegar

75 ml (5 tbsp) tarragon vinegar

150 ml ($\frac{1}{4}$ pint) water

1 shallot, skinned and finely chopped

lemon slices, to garnish

142 ml (5 fl oz) soured cream, to serve

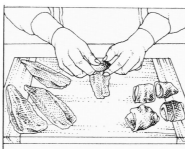

1 Sprinkle the herring fillets with salt and freshly ground pepper and roll up from the head end, skin side outermost.

2 Arrange in a casserole and add the cloves, chillies, peppercorns, bay leaf and mace. Cover with the vinegars and water and sprinkle the shallot on top.

3 Cover and cook in the oven at 170°C (325°F) mark 3 for about 45 minutes or until tender.

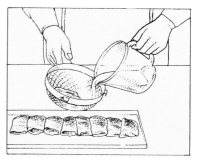

4 Transfer the fish carefully to a serving dish and strain or pour the liquor over. Leave to cool for about 2–3 hours.

5 Garnish the casserole with lemon slices and serve cold with soured cream.

Menu Suggestion

Swedish Herrings make an excellent cold dish for a summer luncheon served with fresh French bread and butter and a selection of salads. Alternatively, halve the quantities given in the recipe and serve for a starter.

SWEDISH HERRINGS

Herrings are inexpensive to buy, yet extremely nutritious. Being oily fish, they are rich in vitamins A and D as well as minerals, and contain almost as much protein as meat. Although they are eaten fresh just as any other oily fish, herrings are immensely popular pickled or soused, especially in northern European and Scandinavian countries where they are a favourite starter. Such herrings are easy to obtain from delicatessens and supermarkets, either loose or in jars (rollmops are a kind of soused herring), but it is so much nicer to make your own using fresh herring fillets as here. For a neat appearance to the finished dish, try to get fillets which are all of an even size and thickness.

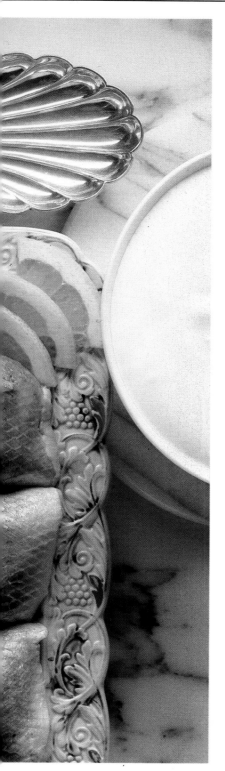

Vegetables

The recipes in this chapter illustrate just how varied and delicious vegetables can be when served as main courses in their own right. They are all suited to vegetarian diets, so you will find them useful and inspiring whenever you have to entertain vegetarians and are unsure what to cook.

In fact they're so tasty and nutritious that non-vegetarians will enjoy them just as much —and probably won't even notice the absence of meat.

Recipes for vegetable accompaniments are on pages 148 to 150.

NIRAMISH (MIXED VEGETABLE CURRY)

| 0.30 | ✳ | 126–168 cals |

Serves 6–8

900 g (2 lb) mixed vegetables (e.g. potatoes, cauliflower, okra, carrots, beans, peas)
60 ml (4 tbsp) vegetable oil
15 ml (1 tbsp) mustard seeds
5 ml (1 tsp) ground cumin
2.5 ml ($\frac{1}{2}$ tsp) ground fenugreek
2 onions, skinned and sliced
2.5 ml ($\frac{1}{2}$ tsp) ground turmeric
salt
2 tomatoes, skinned and chopped
juice of $\frac{1}{2}$ lemon

1 Blanch the vegetables in boiling water. (Potatoes for 10 minutes; cauliflower, okra and carrots for 3 minutes; beans and peas for 2 minutes.) Drain and set the vegetables aside.

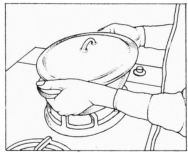

2 Heat the oil in a flameproof casserole, add the mustard seeds, cumin and fenugreek. Cover the casserole and fry gently for 2–3 minutes, shaking the casserole constantly so that the spices do not scorch.

3 Add the onions and turmeric to the spices and fry gently for 5 minutes until the onions soften.

4 Add the vegetables to the pan with salt to taste and moisten with a few spoonfuls of water. Cover the casserole and cook gently for about 5 minutes, stirring occasionally until the vegetables are tender but still crisp.

5 Add the tomatoes and lemon juice and taste and adjust seasoning. Cook for 1 minute more and then turn into a warmed serving dish. Serve hot.

Menu Suggestion
This mixed vegetable curry makes the perfect accompaniment to any meat or poultry main course curry. Alternatively, double the quantities given here and serve as a main course with poppadoms, rice and raita (yogurt).

NIRAMISH
To skin just a few tomatoes as in this recipe, use the following quick method: pierce the tomatoes one at a time in the stalk end with the prongs of a fork. Hold the tomato over a gas flame and twirl in the flame until the skin blisters and bursts on all sides. Remove from the flame and leave until cool enough to handle, then peel off the skin with your fingers—it will come away really easily. Skinning one or two tomatoes this way is quick and simple to do, but it will make all the difference to the appearance and texture of the finished dish.

STUFFED CABBAGE

2.00	🍳 £	205 cals

Serves 4

8–10 large cabbage leaves,
trimmed

30 ml (2 tbsp) vegetable oil

2 onions, skinned and finely
chopped

100 g (4 oz) mushrooms, chopped

50 g (2 oz) long grain rice

450 ml (¾ pint) vegetable or chicken
stock

397 g (14 oz) can tomatoes

5 ml (1 tsp) Worcestershire sauce

2.5 ml (½ tsp) dried basil

salt and freshly ground pepper

50 g (2 oz) hazelnuts, skinned and
chopped

1 Blanch the cabbage leaves in
boiling water for 3–4 minutes.
Drain thoroughly.

2 Heat 15 ml (1 tbsp) of the oil
in a frying pan and fry half
the onions with the mushrooms
for 5 minutes until browned. Add
the rice and stir well.

3 Add 300 ml (½ pint) of the
stock to the rice. Cover and
cook for about 15 minutes until
the rice is tender and the stock
has been absorbed.

4 Meanwhile make a tomato
sauce. Heat the remaining oil
in a pan and fry the remaining
onion for about 5 minutes until
golden. Add the tomatoes, remaining stock, Worcestershire sauce,
basil and seasoning. Bring to the
boil, stirring, and simmer for 8
minutes. Blend until smooth.

5 Stir the hazelnuts into the rice
with seasoning to taste, then
remove from the heat.

6 Divide the rice mixture
between the cabbage leaves
and roll up to make neat parcels.

7 Arrange the cabbage parcels in
an ovenproof dish. Pour over
the tomato sauce.

8 Cover and cook in the oven at
180°C (350°F) mark 4 for
about 1 hour until tender.

Menu Suggestion

These Stuffed Cabbage Rolls
make a delicious vegetarian lunch
or supper served with hot French
bread. Follow with a tomato and
onion salad for a well-balanced
and colourful meal.

STUFFED PEPPERS

| 1.15 | 🎩 | 288 cals |

Serves 6

3 green peppers

3 red peppers

50 g (2 oz) butter

1 onion, skinned and finely
chopped

100 g (4 oz) long grain rice

450 ml (¾ pint) vegetable or chicken
stock

15 ml (1 tbsp) tomato purée

100 g (4 oz) mushrooms, sliced

salt and freshly ground pepper

75 g (3 oz) pine nuts or flaked
almonds, roasted and chopped

10 ml (2 tsp) soy sauce

30 ml (2 tbsp) vegetable oil

4 Season well and stir in the
nuts and soy sauce. Use this
mixture to fill the peppers.

5 Replace lids, then place
peppers in a deep ovenproof
dish and pour over the oil. Cover
and cook in the oven at 190°C
(375°F) mark 5 for 30 minutes
until tender.

Menu Suggestion
With their stuffing of rice,
mushrooms and nuts, these
stuffed peppers are substantial
enough to serve on their own. Hot
garlic or herb bread can be served
with them, if extra carbohydrate is
required.

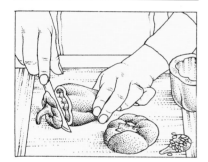

1 Cut a 2.5 cm (1 inch) lid from
the stem end of the peppers.
Scoop out the seeds and membrane. Blanch the shells and lids in
boiling water for about 2 minutes.
Drain and cool.

2 Melt the butter in a saucepan
and gently fry the onion for 5
minutes until softened. Stir in the
rice and cook for 1–2 minutes.

3 Add the stock, tomato purée
and mushrooms. Bring to the
boil and simmer for 13–15
minutes until the rice is tender
and all the stock absorbed.

BARBECUED BEANS

| 4.20* | £ | 213 cals |

* plus overnight soaking

Serves 6

350 g (12 oz) red kidney beans,
    soaked overnight
1.1 litres (2 pints) tomato juice
1 large onion, skinned and sliced
30 ml (2 tbsp) soy sauce
60 ml (4 tbsp) cider vinegar
15 ml (1 tbsp) Worcestershire sauce
15 ml (1 tbsp) mustard powder
15 ml (1 tbsp) honey
2.5 ml ($\frac{1}{2}$ tsp) chilli powder
salt and freshly ground pepper

1 Drain the beans and place in a saucepan. Cover with cold water, bring to the boil and boil rapidly for 10 minutes then drain.

2 Put the tomato juice, onion, soy sauce, vinegar, Worcestershire sauce, mustard, honey and chilli powder in a flameproof casserole. Bring to the boil then add the beans.

3 Cover and cook in the oven at 140°C (275°F) mark 1 for about 4 hours until the beans are tender. Season well with salt and freshly ground pepper.

Menu Suggestion
Serve as a vegetable accompaniment to any roast or grilled meat or poultry.

BUCKWHEAT AND LENTIL CASSEROLE

| 1.45 | 453 cals |

Serves 4

450 ml (¾ pint) water

salt and freshly ground pepper

150 g (5 oz) buckwheat

30 ml (2 tbsp) vegetable oil

1 red or green pepper, cored, seeded and cut into strips

1 onion, skinned and finely chopped

350 g (12 oz) courgettes, trimmed and sliced

175 g (6 oz) mushrooms, sliced

225 g (8 oz) red lentils

3 bay leaves

30 ml (2 tbsp) lemon juice

1 garlic clove, skinned and crushed

2 rosemary sprigs

5 ml (1 tsp) cumin seeds

600 ml (1 pint) vegetable stock

25 g (1 oz) butter

chopped fresh parsley, to garnish

1 Bring the water to the boil in a saucepan, add a pinch of salt, then sprinkle in the buckwheat and return to the boil. Boil rapidly for 1 minute. Reduce the heat, cover and cook gently for 12 minutes or until the water has been absorbed. Do not stir. Transfer to a buttered casserole.

2 Heat the oil in a flameproof casserole and fry the pepper and onion for 5 minutes. Add the courgettes and mushrooms and fry for 5 minutes. Stir in the lentils, bay leaves, lemon juice, garlic, rosemary, cumin and stock. Add to the casserole and stir well.

3 Simmer for about 45 minutes until the lentils are cooked, stirring occasionally. Add the butter, adjust the seasoning and sprinkle with parsley. Serve hot with a bowl of grated cheese, if liked.

Menu Suggestion

Packed with protein, this casserole makes a perfect main course dish for vegetarians, and is especially nutritious if served with boiled brown rice.

VEGETABLE HOT POT

| 1.30 | £ | ✳ | 533 cals |

Serves 4

450 g (1 lb) carrots, peeled and thinly sliced

2 large onions, skinned and thinly sliced

3 celery sticks, trimmed and thinly sliced

450 g (1 lb) potatoes, peeled and sliced

100 g (4 oz) swede, peeled and thinly sliced

450 ml ($\frac{3}{4}$ pint) vegetable stock

bouquet garni

salt and freshly ground pepper

425 g (15 oz) can butter beans, drained

100 g (4 oz) frozen peas

175 g (6 oz) fresh breadcrumbs

175 g (6 oz) hard cheese, grated

1 Layer the carrot, onion, celery, potato and swede in a 2.3 litre (4 pint) casserole.

2 Pour the vegetable stock into the casserole and add the bouquet garni and seasoning.

3 Cover and cook the stock and vegetables in the oven at 180°C (350°F) mark 4 for 1 hour.

4 Remove the bouquet garni. Add the beans and peas to the casserole. Mix the breadcrumbs and cheese together. Spoon over the hot pot. Return to the oven, uncovered, for about 20 minutes.

Menu Suggestion
Vegetable Hotpot makes a delicious winter supper or lunch for the family. Serve with hot French bread and a glass or two of cider or beer.

VEGETABLE HOTPOT
Vegetable stock cubes are now becoming easier to obtain in supermarkets and delicatessens. Shops with kosher departments are likely to stock them, but if you still find them difficult to obtain, simply save the water from cooking vegetables. After straining, boil it until reduced, then store it in the refrigerator as you would meat stock.

SOUTHERN BAKED BEANS

5.40* £ 323 cals

* plus overnight soaking

Serves 4

275 g (10 oz) dried haricot beans, soaked overnight
15 ml (1 tbsp) vegetable oil
2 onions, skinned and chopped
225 g (8 oz) carrots, peeled and chopped
15 ml (1 tbsp) mustard powder
30 ml (2 tbsp) treacle
300 ml ($\frac{1}{2}$ pint) tomato juice
45 ml (3 tbsp) tomato purée
300 ml ($\frac{1}{2}$ pint) beer
salt and freshly ground pepper

1 Drain the beans and place in a saucepan of water. Bring to the boil and simmer for 25 minutes, then drain.

2 Meanwhile, heat the oil in a flameproof casserole and fry the onions and carrots for 5 minutes until lightly golden.

3 Remove from the heat, add the mustard, treacle, tomato juice and purée, beer and beans. Stir well.

4 Bring to the boil, cover and cook in the oven at 140°C (275°F) mark 1 for about 5 hours, stirring occasionally, until the beans are tender and the sauce is the consistency of syrup. Season well with salt and pepper.

Menu Suggestion
Serve these spiced, sweet beans as an accompaniment to roast or barbecued pork. Alternatively, serve them as a vegetarian dish with boiled rice or hot herb bread.

COUSCOUS (NORTH AFRICAN SPICY VEGETABLE STEW)

3.15* 🍽 🍽 620 cals

* plus overnight soaking

Serves 6

450 g (1 lb) couscous

450 ml (¾ pint) tepid water

4 courgettes, trimmed and cut into 1 cm (½ inch) slices

1 red pepper, cored, seeded and diced

1 green pepper, cored, seeded and diced

2 onions, skinned and diced

2 carrots, peeled and diced

225 g (8 oz) turnips, peeled and diced

1 small cauliflower, cut into small florets

4 large tomatoes, skinned and chopped

2 garlic cloves, skinned and crushed

1.1 litres (2 pints) vegetable stock

salt and freshly ground pepper

225 g (8 oz) chick peas, soaked overnight, then drained

25 g (1 oz) blanched almonds

5 ml (1 tsp) ground turmeric

10 ml (2 tsp) paprika

2.5 ml (½ tsp) ground coriander

75 g (3 oz) butter, melted

100 g (4 oz) dried apricots, soaked overnight

1 Place the couscous in a large bowl with the water and leave to soak for 1 hour.

2 Place the prepared vegetables in a large saucepan with the garlic, stock, pepper to taste, chick peas, almonds and spices. Bring to the boil, cover and simmer for 30 minutes.

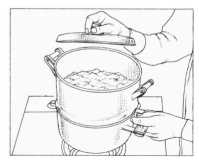

3 Drain the couscous grains and place them in a steamer over the saucepan of vegetables. Cover and continue cooking for a further 40 minutes, then remove steamer and cover saucepan.

4 Place the couscous in a large mixing bowl. Beat the butter into the couscous with 50 ml (2 fl oz) lightly salted water. Leave for 15 minutes.

5 Drain and quarter the apricots, add them to the vegetables and simmer for 15 minutes. Stir the couscous well to remove any lumps and return it to the steamer over the simmering vegetables for 20 minutes, covered.

6 Season the vegetables. Serve vegetables and couscous on a warmed serving dish.

Menu Suggestions
This dish of Couscous comes with its own vegetables and so makes a very substantial main course dish on its own. Serve with hot French bread and follow with a crisp green salad.

USEFUL INFORMATION
AND
BASIC RECIPES

Equipment for Casseroles

The equipment needed to make a casserole is very simple—in most cases only a casserole dish is required, and a few simple pieces of kitchen equipment such as knives, chopping boards, spoons and spatulas. Choose from the equipment on this page according to individual taste and requirements.

A casserole dish is a cooking pot with a tight-fitting lid and two handles, designed to cook food slowly. Casserole dishes come in a variety of shapes, sizes and materials and may be flameproof or just ovenproof. They are also used as serving dishes as most casseroles are served straight from their cooking pot.

As with most cooking equipment it is worth investing in a good casserole dish which will be efficient, hard-wearing and attractive. There are several points which should be taken into consideration when choosing one to suit your needs.

The dish itself should be sturdy and sufficiently heavy so that foods will not stick to the bottom and burn during the long cooking process. The lid must also fit well to conserve the moisture and prevent evaporation. For this reason casseroles have straight, deep sides and some, such as the French 'marmite', slope inwards towards the top to prevent evaporation.

The handles are usually made of the same material as the pot so that they are ovenproof. They should be small enough to fit in the oven, yet easy to grip when the casserole is full and hot. The best dishes for cooking are thick and heavy, but remember that they can be extremely difficult to lift when full, especially when cooking large quantities.

It is useful to have several casseroles of different shapes and sizes to suit your cooking needs and numbers to cater for. The dishes are usually round but oval casseroles can be useful for cooking large joints or poultry. They range in size from individual portions to party sizes for twenty or more servings. Ideally, the dish should not be less than half-full to prevent the food from drying out.

Casserole dishes are available in many shapes, sizes and materials

Useful pieces of equipment for preparing casseroles

TYPES OF CASSEROLE DISHES

The major differences between dishes are due to the materials from which they are made:

Aluminium: Seldom used for casseroles as the handles of pans are often not ovenproof, but it makes economical flameproof pots. Some foods and hard water can leave stains.

Copper: Makes very expensive but attractive casseroles. However, they must be lined to prevent reaction with foods and need frequent cleaning. Copper is a very good heat conductor and therefore ideal for the initial frying of foods.

Earthenware: Earthenware or stoneware can be glazed or unglazed and come in a wide variety of shapes and sizes. While they look very attractive, most are not flameproof and can easily break.

Enamelled cast iron: This is a very popular material for flameproof casseroles as they are medium priced and look attractive with their brightly coloured finishes. They are however, very heavy, especially when full.

Glass: Ovenproof or flameproof. Its main advantage is that it is see-through, but it is also breakable.

Porcelain: Attractive-looking but delicate and only ovenproof.

Stainless steel: Although more common for saucepans, stainless steel is also a useful material for casseroles which can then double as a saucepan as well. It is a very tough, durable metal with a shiny finish that is easy to keep clean and impervious to acids and alkalis. It should be fairly thick to prevent burning, with a base of copper or aluminium to conduct the heat well. Care must be taken in handling as the handles can get very hot. Good-quality pots are very expensive.

Since casseroles are usually served straight from the cooking dish, it is also important that the dishes be attractive and if possible match other tableware and serving dishes. They should also be easy to clean and dishwasher-proof if that is a consideration.

Casserole dishes can be divided into two types: ovenproof and flameproof. Flameproof casseroles, although they may not look as attractive as the ovenproof varieties, are much more versatile pieces of equipment. They have the advantage that they can be used for the initial frying as well as subsequent cooking of the casserole, which saves on the washing up of frying pans. They can also double up as saucepans which can be taken straight to the table. (A casserole may also be cooked on the hob throughout over a very gentle heat.)

The material from which the dish is made determines many of its properties—such as whether it is flameproof, a good conductor of heat, breakable, easy to clean, heavy to lift, etc. Flameproof casseroles are made from metal such as stainless steel, aluminium, copper and enamelled iron. Ovenproof casseroles are made from heat-resistant glass, porcelain and earthenware (some of these materials may also be treated to make them flameproof but care must still be taken with high and sudden heats). Non-stick linings can also be applied to the insides to prevent the food sticking and eliminate the need for fat to be used for cooking.

If a casserole dish is not available, a saucepan with a heavy base and tight-fitting lid may be used instead over a gentle heat.

A casserole may also be cooked in an electric slow cooker which allows for very long, slow cooking, and which can be left unattended while you are out. In the other extreme, a casserole can be cooked very quickly in a pressure cooker or microwave oven, but as these techniques are very different the manufacturer's instructions must be followed carefully.

OTHER EQUIPMENT

Apart from a casserole dish, a frying pan or saucepan may also be needed to fry the meat first or make the sauce. Other useful pieces of equipment include sharp knives and chopping boards, wooden spoons, perforated spoons, slices and tongs.

Preparation and Cooking Techniques

Casseroles are some of the easiest dishes to prepare, cook and serve; and because they are so 'good tempered' are perfect for busy cooks.

Although they can take a long time to cook, the preparation is quick and uncomplicated and can be carried out well in advance. In fact, casseroles usually improve on reheating and will happily wait until you are ready.

The simplest casseroles just require the ingredients to be prepared and placed in the dish and then they will cook themselves. They are also ideal for freezing and reheating.

COOKING TECHNIQUES

All casseroles are cooked by a long, slow, moist cooking process. There are three basic methods:

FRY START METHOD
(BROWN CASSEROLES)
This is the most common method, which seals in juices and gives the casserole a good colour. It can be used for all cuts of meat, poultry, fish and vegetables (except for very tough and bony cuts of meat which would be further toughened by the initial frying process).

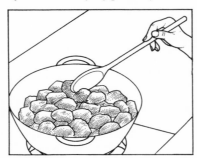

Frying prepared meat until browned

The prepared meat is fried in a little fat until browned on all sides, using a flameproof casserole, frying pan or large saucepan. Any cooking fats or oils may be used for the frying, the most common being corn oil, olive oil, butter, lard or polyunsaturated fats and oils. If using butter it is a good idea to add a little oil to prevent it from burning. If using a non-stick pan, a minimum amount of fat can

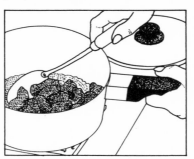

Removing meat from pan after frying

be used. The meat is usually removed from the pan with a slice, or a wooden or metal spoon and drained on a plate lined with absorbent kitchen paper.

The prepared vegetables are then added to the pan to be fried (the same fat can be used unless it has burnt, in which case it should be renewed). Onions are usually added for their flavour and may be chopped or sliced or, if button onions are used, left whole. (Chopped bacon can also be added at this stage for extra flavour.) Other vegetables used will depend on the sort of recipe and season, but may include carrot, celery, turnip, swede, parsnip, red and green peppers (other vegetables which do not take long to cook may be added towards the end of the cooking time). Spices and flavourings which are best fried such as garlic, root ginger, curry spices and paprika are also added at this stage of preparation.

Stirring in flour to absorb fat

A little flour is often stirred into the fried vegetables to absorb the fat and thicken the casserole (some of the flour may be used to toss the meat before frying to help brown it). The flour may be fried gently until brown in colour to give a brown sauce.

The liquid, which may be water, stock, red or white wine, cider or beer, is then stirred in and brought to the boil, stirring until the sauce is smooth and slightly thickened (the sauce will get thinner on cooking as the juices run out of the meat).

Return the fried meat to the pot

(if using a flameproof casserole) or transfer the meat to an ovenproof casserole dish and pour over the vegetables and sauce. Other flavourings can now be added such as seasonings, herbs, fresh or canned tomatoes or tomato purée, fruits such as apple slices, grated rind and juice of oranges and lemons, pineapple chunks, dried fruit, pre-soaked or cooked pulses, nuts and seeds. The list of ingredients that can be added to a casserole is endless, producing a wide variety of different flavours, textures and colours.

The pot should then be covered tightly and simmered very gently until the meat is tender. The casserole can be cooked in a slow to medium oven, or on top of the cooker where it will need occasional watching to make sure it does not dry out. The cooking time will depend on the type of food and toughness of the meat, but may be 30 minutes for fish, 1 hour for poultry and from 2 to 4 hours for meat.

Towards the end of cooking, other flavourings can be added: vegetables such as courgettes, peas, mushrooms; fruits such as grapes, cherries, bananas; toppings such as dumplings, breadcrumbs, grated or sliced cheese; chopped fresh herbs.

If the casserole has not been thickened with flour by this stage, it may be thickened just before serving with cornflour or arrow-root (which gives a translucent sauce). A little of the powder

Thickening with cornflour

should be 'slaked' with some cold water in a basin to dissolve it, stirred into the hot liquid and then cooked until thickened. Flour may also be added just before serving if mixed to a paste with softened butter (called 'beurre manié') and stirred into the hot liquid in small pieces. More exotic and complicated dishes can be thickened with egg yolk before serving, but care must be taken not to curdle the sauce.

Cream, soured cream and yogurt can be stirred into the casserole before serving but, to prevent curdling, should not be allowed to boil. Seasonings and other flavourings can also be added to taste before serving.

Once cooked the casserole can be kept warm in a cool oven until required. It may also be made in advance, cooled and refrigerated or frozen before being reheated.

COLD START METHOD
(WHITE CASSEROLES)

This all-in-one method of cooking casseroles is used specifically to tenderise the tougher cuts of meat, although it may be used for more tender cuts of meat, poultry, fish and vegetables.

It is often more convenient and time-saving to put all the ingredients into one pot without the initial frying of the meat and vegetables. This is especially useful when using ovenproof casserole dishes, as no other pans are then needed.

The same ingredients can be

Adding layers of vegetables

used as with the fry start method and they are simply placed in the casserole dish in layers. The cold liquid is then poured over, allowing no more than 300 ml ($\frac{1}{2}$ pint) liquid to 450 g (1 lb) of meat and this proportion should be reduced when increasing the quantity of meat. Cover the dish and place in a slow to moderate oven and cook until the meat is tender. The cooking time will be considerably longer than with the fry start method. This gradual heating of the liquid softens the meat fibres and allows the juices to run out, producing a rich-flavoured gravy.

Once the meat is tender it may be treated as the fry start casserole as far as additions, flavourings and thickenings are concerned.

BRAISING OR POT-ROASTING METHOD

Casseroles can also be cooked by braising or pot-roasting. This method of cooking is usually used for larger pieces of meat and whole birds or fish.

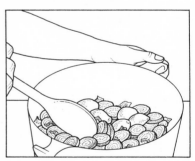

Browning vegetables

The meat is usually browned first and then removed from the pan while the vegetables are then browned. The meat is placed on top of the vegetables, a small amount of liquid may be added and then the casserole is covered and cooked in a moderate oven. The meat is kept very moist by cooking in its own juices and is well flavoured from the bed of vegetables. The meat may be served with or without the vegetables, or the vegetables may be puréed to form a sauce.

THICKENING FOR CASSEROLES

Thickening casseroles ensures a smooth texture and holds heavy ingredients in suspension.

Plain flour, potato flour, corn-flour and arrowroot are used in the proportion of 25 g (1 oz) thickening agent to 600 ml (1 pint) of liquid.

How to add thickenings and liaisons—

Flours and other powdered cereals: Mix smoothly with a little cold liquid, then add just before serving and boil for at least 5 minutes, stirring gently all the time.

Egg: The richer white meat or fish casseroles may be thickened by eggs or egg yolks beaten with a little cream, milk or white stock. Just before serving, add

Adding beaten egg mixture to thicken

about 30–45 ml (2–3 table-spoons) of the hot but not boiling liquid to the beaten egg mixture, then stir this into the contents of the casserole (which should be not quite boiling). Cook and stir for a few minutes by the side of the heat, in order to form the liaison, but do not boil or the egg may curdle.

Beurre manié (butter and flour): This provides a quick method of thickening casseroles. Knead together 25 g (1 oz) plain flour and 25 g (1 oz) butter to thicken 600 ml (1 pint) of liquid; add this a small piece at a time to the hot liquid, whisking all the time, then bring to boiling point.

PREPARATION OF MEAT

BUYING

Almost any cut of meat may be used for casseroles, but the long, slow, moist cooking is particularly suited to cheaper cuts of meat to make them tender. The meat may be minced, cut up into bite-sized or single portion pieces, served as chops or steaks or even large joints. Fresh or frozen meat may be used, although it is best to defrost frozen meat first.

Allow 100–175 g (4–6 oz) of boneless meat per person, depend-ing on appetites and the quantities of vegetables and other ingredients in the recipe. For meat on the bone you should allow about 225 g (8 oz) per person.

STORAGE

Store fresh meat in a refrigerator or cold place and use as soon as possible after purchase. It should be wrapped loosely in polythene bags, cling film or foil to prevent it drying out or the juices leaking out, or the transfer of food smells. It is often advisable to place meat on a plate or tray to prevent the juices leaking out on to other foods in the refrigerator. Mince should be cooked on the same day as it is bought, small cuts up to two days later and large joints up to three days later if refrigerated.

For longer storage, buy frozen meat and store in the freezer, or freeze fresh meat yourself. Store for about six months in the freezer.

PREPARATION

Wipe the meat with a clean, damp cloth or paper towel. Dry de-frosted, frozen meat well.

If necessary trim off any surplus fat, skin or gristle, and cut off bones if desired.

Cut the meat as required for the recipe using a sharp knife on a chopping board. The meat may be

Cutting meat into cubes

cut into small or large cubes, strips or shreds or cut into single portion pieces. Single portions of meat can be flattened to make escalopes (place between two sheets of greaseproof paper and beat with a rolling pin) then stuffed and rolled and secured with string or cocktail sticks. Chops and steaks may be slit to form a pocket which can then be stuffed. Large joints may be left on the bone, boned, rolled and stuffed or cut up into smaller pieces.

SUITABLE CUTS OF MEAT FOR CASSEROLING

Beef	leg, shin, chuck, flank, blade, skirt, joints of topside, top rump, brisket, silverside
Lamb	breast, scrag, middle or best end of neck, loin. Shoulder and leg may be cooked as joints or boned and cubed
Pork	hand, sparerib, belly (trimmed of fat). Also loin chops, spare rib chops and fillet. Gammon steaks and joints and cooked, cubed ham
Veal	breast, neck, shoulder, shin, leg, knuckle

MARINADES

After preparation the meat can be left to soak in a marinade before it is cooked, to tenderise it and add various flavourings.

Marinades usually consist of a mixture of liquids including wine, vinegar, oil, citrus fruit juices, natural yogurt; and flavourings such as herbs and spices and raw chopped vegetables like onion and garlic. The acids in the marinade break down the tough connective tissue in the meat and the oil adds succulence. The marinade is usually added to the cooking liquid so that the flavours penetrate the meat during cooking as well.

Meat can be left to marinate at room temperature for several hours, or overnight and up to 3 days in the refrigerator.

PREPARATION OF VARIETY MEATS (OFFAL)

Offal covers a wide variety of meats, including liver, kidney, heart, sweetbreads, tripe, tongue, brains, oxtail, sausages. All these meats can be used to make delicious casseroles.

BUYING

Most offal is an economical buy, especially as there is little waste from bones, gristle or fat.

The more common varieties such as liver and kidney can be bought fresh, but less popular types such as sweetbreads or brains are often sold frozen and may even have to be ordered in advance.

Allow 100–175 g (4–6 oz) of offal per person (small portions are usually sufficient as offal tends to be very rich).

VARIETIES AND PREPARATION

Brains: Lamb's and calf's brains are the most common and need pre-soaking and cooking as for sweetbreads to make them firm and white (see page 136).

To prepare, they should be soaked in cold water for at least 1 hour. Drain and carefully remove as much skin and membrane as possible using scissors, and pull out the red veins. Place the brains in a pan, cover with acidulated

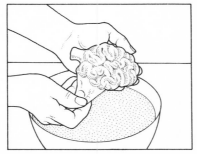

Removing skin from brains

water and simmer for 15 minutes. Drain and leave to cool until firm when any remaining skin and veins can be removed.

They have a very soft, smooth texture and do not take very long to cook.

Heart *(lamb, pig, ox)*: Heart is more like lean meat in flavour and texture than other types of offal. It is ideal to casserole as it has a dense, muscular texture which needs long, slow cooking to become tender.

Lamb's hearts are the smallest and most popular with a mild

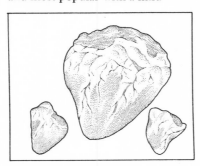

Pig's, ox and lamb's hearts

flavour and are often stuffed and braised to serve one per person. Pig's hearts are a little bigger and ox heart is very large—up to about 1.8 kg (4 lb)—with a coarse texture and strong flavour; ox heart is always cut up before cooking.

To prepare, remove the tubes and gristle and soak in cold water.

Kidney *(lamb, pig, ox, calf)*: Fresh kidneys are sold individually with the layer of white suet already removed. Frozen kidneys are usually sold by weight.

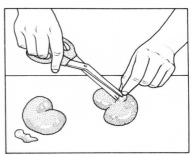

Coring kidneys

To prepare kidneys, peel off the inner thin skin. Cut in half through the white core and remove the core by snipping out with scissors.

Lamb's and pig's kidneys can be cooked in halves or cut into slices. Calf and ox kidney are bigger with many lobes and should be cut into slices or small pieces.

Ox kidney is the most common to use in stews and is often sold already cut up for steak and kidney pie. It has a stronger flavour and needs longer cooking than the other kidneys.

Liver (*calf, lamb, pig, ox, chicken and turkey*): The different types vary considerably in price, flavour and texture. Calf and lamb's liver are very tender but toughen with prolonged cooking, whereas pig and ox liver improve with long cooking. To prepare, cut into thin, even slices and remove any thin membrane or skin. Minced pig's liver is often used for stuffings, pâtés or meatballs such as faggots.

Oxtail: Oxtail is usually sold skinned and jointed. One large

Joints of oxtail

oxtail should be enough for 4 people and is about 2 kg (4½ lb) in weight. It needs very long, slow cooking to make it tender but gives a delicious rich flavour to winter soups and stews (it is often not readily available in the summer due to lack of demand). It is usually very fatty and therefore it is best to cook it in advance and skim off the fat before reheating.

Sausages: There is a wide variety of traditional and spicy sausages which can be cooked in casseroles. They are very easy to cook and need no special preparation. They may be left whole or sliced; and fried first or added straight to the pot.

Sweetbreads: These are of two types, coming in pairs: the 'throat' or thymus gland, and the 'stomach'

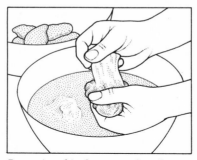

Removing skin from sweetbreads

or pancreas gland which are slightly bigger and coarser. The small lamb's and larger calf's sweetbreads are most widely available and are often sold frozen.

To prepare, sweetbreads must be soaked in cold water for at least 1 hour (this keeps them white by extracting any blood). They should then be precooked to firm them. Drain and cover the sweetbreads with fresh water and 15 ml (1 tbsp) lemon juice or vinegar in a saucepan. Bring to the boil and simmer for 5 minutes. Drain and remove any bits of skin or tissue. They are then ready to use.

Tongue: Ox tongue is the most common and is very large, about 1.8 kg (4 lb) in weight. It is usually cooked whole and sliced or pressed and served as a cold meat. It may be sold fresh or salted, in which case it should be soaked in cold water for several hours or overnight to reduce the saltiness. It

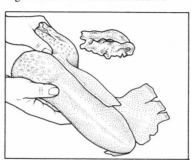

Peeling skin from ox tongue

takes several hours cooking in water and flavourings to make it tender and is therefore ideal to casserole. When tender the skin can be peeled off.

Lamb's tongues are much smaller, about 100–225 g (4–8 oz) each and are usually served hot. Calf's tongue is in between in size and flavour and may be served hot or cold.

Tripe: Tripe is the stomach lining, usually of ox. There are

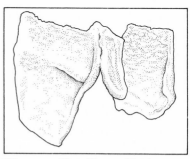

'Honeycomb' and 'smooth' tripe

two types: the smooth 'blanket' from the first stomach and the 'honeycomb' from the second stomach. Both should be firm, thick and white and are sold 'dressed' (cleaned and par-boiled). Even though precooked, tripe still needs fairly long, slow cooking to soften, so casseroling is ideal. It has a very mild flavour.

Other types of offal: Other less common types of meat come under the heading of offal such as whole heads, ears of pig, calf and sheep, cow heel, calf's foot, pig's trotters. All these can be casseroled and are valuable for their gelatinous stock.

STORAGE
Offal does not keep well and preferably should be used on the same day as purchase. It should be stored loosely covered in the refrigerator and can be soaked in a bowl of cold water to remove any taints of blood. Fresh offal may also be stored in the freezer for three months.

PREPARATION OF POULTRY

All types of poultry can be casseroled, and this cooking method makes the meat very moist and tender (whereas other methods of cooking such as roasting can dry out the meat because it is so lean).

Birds can be casseroled whole but are more often jointed, which makes serving much easier than carving at the table. Poultry can be prepared in advance and reheated when required, which is useful on numerous occasions.

BUYING
Most poultry is sold ready for cooking, i.e., hung, plucked, drawn and trussed. It may be fresh, chilled (stored just above freezing) or frozen. Birds should be sold with their giblets, but beware as some chilled and frozen birds come without (a stock made from the giblets improves the flavour of a casserole enormously).

Chicken: The most common chicken available in the shops is a roasting chicken but this is also suitable for casseroles. It may be sold as a whole bird or cut into quarters or smaller joints. In supermarkets it is also possible to

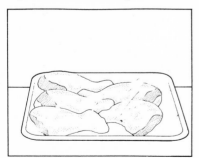

Ready-prepared chicken joints

buy joints all of the same type e.g. a packet of chicken breasts or thighs or drumsticks, which makes a wide variety of chicken 'cuts' available.

Boiling fowl are now hard to come by, but are ideal for casseroling as they are older, tougher birds which become tender with long, slow cooking. They have an excellent flavour and are considerably cheaper than 'roasting' chickens.

Poussins (baby chickens) which serve one person each, and poulets (spring chickens) which serve two people may also be casseroled, but they are very tender and do not take long to cook.

Poulardes (neutered young hens) and capons (neutered young cocks) are considerably fatter than ordinary chickens and also good in casseroles. As they are larger it is usually more convenient to cut them into joints before cooking, or precook them and take the meat off the bones before making into a casserole.

Duck: Like chicken, is sold fresh, chilled and frozen, and usually as a whole bird, but some supermarkets sell fresh or frozen duck portions. A whole duck is awkward to carve and as a plain roast is often not enough to serve four people. However, cut into quarters

Quartering duck

and casseroled with other ingredients a duck will easily serve four people.

Duck is very fatty so it is often advisable to roast it so that the fat melts out before it is cut up and made into a casserole.

Goose: This bird is seldom used in casseroles as it is too large for most dishes, even if cut into portions. It is more likely to be precooked and the flesh taken off the bones before being made into a casserole.

Guinea fowl: These taste like slightly 'gamey' chicken and are about the size of spring chickens. They tend to be rather dry and cooking in a casserole makes them more moist.

Turkey: This bird is also too large to casserole, but it is possible to buy fresh and frozen turkey joints in supermarkets. Turkey drumsticks make good casseroles and so do breast escalopes which can be stuffed and rolled. It is also a good meat to use precooked and taken off the bone. The best quality fresh turkeys are available at Christmas time.

STORAGE
Fresh poultry should be stored in a cold place or refrigerator. Remove the giblets from inside the bird and keep separately. Wrap the bird loosely or place in a covered dish in the refrigerator. Fresh poultry may also be frozen and stored in the freezer (up to 12 months for chicken and 6 months for other poultry).

Frozen poultry is best defrosted slowly in the refrigerator, which will take overnight or 15 hours depending on the size. Any bird larger than 2.7 kg (6 lb) is best defrosted at room temperature, since it would take too long in the refrigerator. Joints will take about 6 hours to defrost in the refrigerator. It is very important to defrost poultry completely before cooking so that it will be thoroughly cooked through to destroy any bacteria. Poultry should be thawed in its wrappings on a plate or tray, in order to catch the juices.

PREPARATION
Wipe the poultry with a clean, damp cloth or rinse in cold water and dry. Defrosted poultry will need to be dried well.

Make sure that giblets are removed from whole birds. Whole birds may be trussed with string to keep them a good shape and easy to carve. Larger birds may still

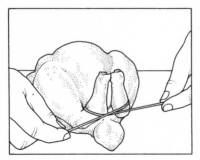

Trussing poultry

have a few feathers and hairs remaining from plucking. These may be removed with tweezers or by singeing (hold the bird over an open flame, turning it quickly).

Whole birds may be stuffed with a sausagemeat, breadcrumb or rice mixture. It is usual to stuff

Stuffing neck end of bird

the neck end, loosely so that the skin will not burst, and then tuck the flap of neck skin over the stuffing and secure under the wings. The cavity of birds may also be stuffed or just flavoured with a knob of butter, peeled onion and sprigs of herbs. Stuffing may also be spread between the skin and flesh of the breast.

It is usually more convenient to cut poultry into joints for casseroles. Small birds may be cut in half through the breastbone and backbone using a large, sharp knife or poultry shears. Slightly larger birds may be cut into quarters, dividing between the legs and breasts. Larger birds may be cut into joints making six to twelve 'cuts' of meat: cut off the legs where they join the carcass, then cut off the wings together

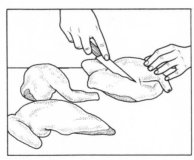

Dividing poultry into portions

with a portion of breast meat. Cut either side of the breastbone to give two breast portions, and discard the breastbone and backbone. These six portions may then be further divided if wished.

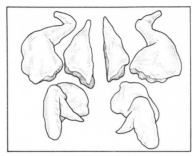

Poultry divided into six joints

A slit may be cut in the breasts to form a pocket for stuffing, and chicken drumsticks can be boned and stuffed.

Poultry may be skinned or cooked with its skin on. If the meat is fried first before putting into the casserole the skin will be nicely browned and crispy. If making a cold start casserole it can be nicer to remove the skin first.

If larger birds are to be precooked so that the meat can be taken off the bone and cut up before making into a casserole, they can be roasted or boiled. Boiling the poultry in water flavoured with vegetables, herbs and giblets makes the meat particularly moist and well flavoured, and you are also left with a delicious stock for making the sauce and other dishes. It is always worth cooking the giblets in a little water for stock for the sauce.

PREPARATION OF FISH AND SHELLFISH

Fish make delicious and versatile casserole dishes, encompassing both fish soups and stews. They differ from meat casseroles in that they are not designed to make the fish tender by long, slow cooking but they ensure that the fish is moist and absorbs other flavours. This is very useful for making bland fish into exotic dishes.

BUYING

There is a wide variety of fish available, both in fishmongers and supermarkets, fresh or frozen.

Depending on the type of fish and individual recipes, fish may be bought in many different forms. It can be a whole fish including the head and tail; a piece of a whole, large fish; fish steaks (on the bone) and fish fillets (boned and sometimes skinned).

Fish is usually sold by weight but some shellfish such as scallops are sold individually. Whole fish are considerably cheaper per pound but do not forget that you are also paying for the wasted parts and the more expensive fillets may work out cheaper.

Buy fish when it is in season and therefore at its best and cheapest. Always buy fish which are absolutely fresh—look for a bright colour with shiny, silvery scales, firm flesh, bright, bulging eyes and a clean, fresh smell.

Allow 100–325 g (4–12 oz) of fish per person, depending on the type of fish and whether it includes bones, heads, guts etc. A medium-sized whole fish of about 225 g (8 oz) will serve 1 person. If there are lots of other ingredients in the casserole less fish will be necessary. Oily fish is more rich and filling than white fish.

For most fish casseroles, the fish specified in the recipe can usually be substituted by another fish of a similar type.

TYPES OF FISH

Flatfish (*brill, sole, halibut, plaice, turbot*): have white fine flesh with a delicate flavour. Sole and plaice are available whole or as fillets. Turbot is prized for its firm flesh, and is usually sold in steaks. Brill and halibut make cheaper substitutes for turbot.

Round White Fish (*bass, bream, cod, coley, conger eel, dog fish, haddock, hake, monkfish, mullet (red and grey), snapper, skate, whiting*): bass, bream, mullet and snapper are usually cooked whole. Cod, sold as steaks or fillets, is a good choice for casseroles; coley and whiting are cheaper substitutes. Conger eel and monkfish both have firm flesh very suitable for casseroling.

Oily Fish (*herring, mackerel, tuna*): herring and mackerel are usually cooked whole. Tuna is sold in steaks. Though seldom found fresh in this country, it is common in cans and its firm texture is suitable for casseroles.

Freshwater Fish (*eel, salmon, sea trout, trout*): eels have a rich meaty texture, ideal for casseroles. Salmon is a prized fish, in season during the summer months. It can be dry, and moist methods of cooking are therefore recommended. Sea trout is a smaller, less expensive substitute for salmon.

Shellfish (*crab, crawfish, crayfish, Dublin Bay prawns (scampi), lobster, mussels, octopus and squid, oysters, prawns and shrimps, scallops*): may be casseroled on their own, but are often added to other fish casseroles for their colour and flavour. Mussels and octopus are both popular in Mediterranean casseroles. Crayfish, prawns and scallops all make colourful, flavoursome additions to casseroles. Oysters were once a traditional British ingredient in beef stews but they are now an expensive delicacy.

STORAGE

In theory fish should never be stored, as it should be cooked and eaten as soon as it is purchased. However, if fish has to be stored it should be covered in the coldest part of the refrigerator, or surrounded by ice. Ideally, fish should be cooked on the same day as purchase, but if it has to be kept overnight, remove the guts and clean the fish well before wrapping in clean paper or film.

Once fish has been cooked and made up into a casserole it may be cooled quickly and stored in the refrigerator, covered overnight and reheated before serving.

Ideally, frozen fish should be defrosted before cooking and this can be done in the refrigerator or more quickly at room temperature.

PREPARATION

Most fishmongers will prepare the fish for you or you may do it yourself. This involves cleaning the fish, which may then be left whole or skinned and filleted or cut into steaks.

CLEANING

Scaling: Some fish have scales which should be removed before cooking. Scrape the blunt edge of

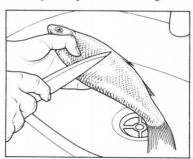

Scaling round fish

a knife along the fish from tail to head (this can be very messy so do it over the sink or sheets of paper). Rinse off the scales under the tap.

Gutting: Round fish: using a sharp knife or scissors make a slit along the belly from the gills towards the tail (if the fish is to be

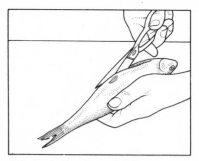

Slitting belly of round fish

left whole make as small a slit as possible). Pull out innards with your fingers. Rinse the fish under

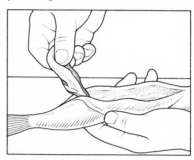

Gutting round fish

cold, running water until completely clean. Flat fish: make a slit just behind the head under the gills and clean in the same way.

Gutting flat fish

Cut off the fins and gills. If the fish is to be cooked whole the head and tail may be left on or off. Rinse in cold water then dry.

SKINNING

Round fish are usually cooked with their skin on but it is also possible to skin them raw: with a sharp knife, slit the skin down the backbone, loosen the skin round the head and peel it off towards the tail. Turn over and repeat.

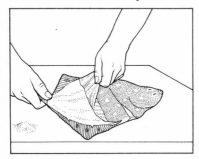

Skinning whole round fish

For whole flat fish: cut the skin across above the tail on the dark skin side. Slip your thumb in the slit just under the skin and carefully loosen the skin round the sides of the fish.

Hold the fish firmly by the tail and pull the skin off quickly towards the head in one piece.

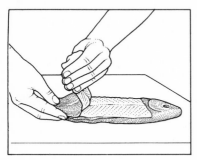

Skinning whole flat fish

(Salt on your fingers will prevent them from slipping.) Usually only the dark skin is removed but the process may be repeated with the other side.

Fillets of fish may be skinned by placing on a board, skin side down. Hold the tail firmly and with a sharp knife cut just above the skin sawing from side to side and pressing the flat of the blade against the flesh. Work towards

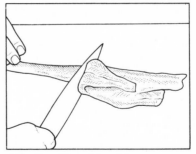

Skinning fillet of flat fish

the head end until the skin is removed—it should come off in one piece.

FILLETING

Round fish are usually filleted before skinning. Cut off the head. Cut along the centre of the back through the flesh to the bone, from the head to the tail, and cut along the belly of the fish. Remove

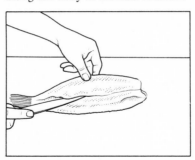

Filleting round fish

the fillet working from the head down, pressing the knife against the bones and using short, slicing movements. Remove the fillet from the other side in the same way. Small round fish such as herring may be boned but with the head and tail left intact; or with the head and tail removed to give one fillet: slit the fish open along the belly and remove the innards. Open out the fish so that all the skin is facing upwards. Press firmly with fingers along the centre of the back to loosen the backbone. Turn the fish over and

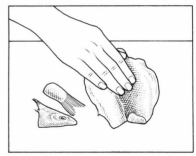

Loosening backbone of round fish

ease up the backbone in one piece. Reshape the fish if it is to be left whole, or roll up towards tail, or cut into two fillets.

Flat fish are usually cut into four fillets, two from each side. Lay the unskinned fish flat on a board and cut through the flesh to the backbone along the length of the fish. Cut away a fillet from one

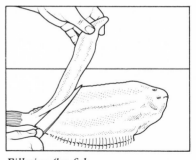

Filleting flat fish

side of the backbone with a sharp knife using short, sharp movements and repeat with the other side. Turn fish over and repeat.

SHELLFISH

All shellfish needs very careful cleaning and preparation and this is often done by the fishmonger.

All live shellfish must be boiled before using in a recipe: boil in salted water for 5 to 30 minutes depending on type of fish.

Most shellfish have indigestible or inedible parts such as 'beards', gills, intestines and stomach which must be removed. Shells must also be removed to expose the meat.

FREEZING

Not only do casseroles freeze and reheat extremely well, but most of them improve by being made in advance and reheated. This makes casserole cookery very versatile and convenient and allows the dishes to be prepared to suit you. If casseroles are frozen and stored correctly they should come out of the freezer in the same condition as they went in. There are a few basic rules which must be followed for successful freezing.

The raw ingredients for casseroles may also be frozen, such as meat, poultry and game, and these should be thawed before cooking in a casserole. Frozen food which has defrosted should not be refrozen as this could allow the micro-organisms to multiply rapidly. However, raw food which has been defrosted may be thoroughly cooked in a casserole and then refrozen.

COOKING CASSEROLES FOR THE FREEZER

When cooking casseroles for the freezer it is a good idea to make them in bulk. This saves labour, time and fuel. It is always a waste to have the oven on for several hours while cooking a casserole, so try and cook other dishes in the oven at the same time. If you are cooking a casserole to be served immediately or the next day, why not make up a double quantity and freeze half of it for future use?

Nearly all casseroles can be frozen. The only exceptions are casseroles which include eggs, cream or yogurt which would curdle on reheating; and highly spiced and seasoned casseroles which tend to produce a 'musty' flavour after several weeks of storage in the freezer. This is particularly true of garlic, so it is best to add most strong spices and flavourings on reheating the casserole after it has been frozen; or alternatively only freeze these casseroles for a short time.

Casseroles thickened with flour tend to thin down on freezing, so be prepared to rethicken the sauce after reheating. Garnishes and last-minute additions such as cream should be omitted until after the casserole has been reheated for serving.

Good hygiene is very important when preparing foods for the freezer (freezing does not kill germs and any present in the food would be activated again on thawing and rapidly multiply), so make sure that all working surroundings are scrupulously clean.

If freezer space is at a premium, do not waste space by preparing a casserole with meat that contains a high proportion of bones.

When making the sauce, be generous with the quantities of liquid as the food should be submerged in liquid during freezing.

Undercook the casserole before freezing to allow for extra cooking time on reheating. This is especially important for casseroles which do not take long to cook such as fish and vegetables. It is also possible to prepare or pre-fry the food and pour over the sauce and freeze the casserole at this stage before it is cooked. Delicate foods such as fish, which might fall apart when transferred to and from containers and dishes, can be arranged on the dish in which they will be reheated and served and frozen on this (as long as the dish is freezer-proof and sufficiently wrapped).

It is also useful to freeze stocks so that they are available in the

Packing cubes of frozen stock

freezer when you are making casseroles. Concentrated stock can be frozen in ice cube trays and then packed in polythene bags, and just one or two of these stock cubes can be added to a casserole sauce without defrosting first.

It is very important that after cooking, the casserole should be cooled as quickly as possible (to prevent organisms from multiplying) and that the casserole should be completely cold before packing in the freezer. To speed up the

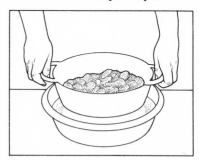

Cooling casserole before freezing

cooling process, the dish may be placed in a bowl of iced water.

FREEZER CONTAINERS AND WRAPPINGS

Foods must be well protected while they are stored in the freezer and containers must be moisture and vapour proof. Freezing will draw out moisture from unprotected foods resulting in 'freezer burn'.

Aluminium foil: This can be used for wrapping casseroles but as they contain liquid, can be rather messy. Use heavy-duty freezer foil, or ordinary foil, doubled, and use to line a rigid container which can be removed when the food is solid. Larger pieces of meat or poultry can be wrapped in foil while the sauce is frozen in a carton separately. Foil punctures easily so it is advisable to overwrap it in polythene. Foil may be re-used, but only if handled with care and if not punctured. If not re-used it becomes expensive.

Casserole dishes: These can be used for freezing as long as they are freezer-proof and will not crack, and can be properly sealed. Some flameproof dishes allow the casserole to be fried, cooked, frozen and reheated all in the same dish. They do however, take up a lot of valuable space in the freezer, are heavy and difficult to stack for storing in the freezer, and also are not then available for cooking other foods. Alternatively, a

Lining casserole dish with foil

casserole dish may be lined with freezer foil or polythene before freezing the food; when the food is frozen solid, it can be removed from the dish and wrapped for storage in the freezer, thus releasing the dish for further use.

Foil containers with lids: These are convenient for freezing casseroles as they can also be used for

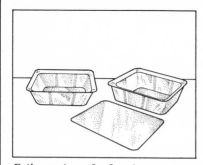
Foil containers for freezing

reheating. They are easy to store in the freezer and can be washed and re-used.

Polythene bags: These are very versatile, but they should be of the heavy duty type. Pouring casseroles into a bag can be messy unless the bag is first placed inside

Packing casserole into polythene bag

a rigid container which can be removed when food is solid. All air should be excluded from the bag before securing with wire ties, string or elastic bands or freezer tape. Polythene bags can also be used for overwrapping other dishes. They may be washed and re-used if not punctured.

Polythene boxes: These come in a variety of shapes and sizes and are very useful for freezing casseroles; they should have airtight lids. Square and oblong rigid con-

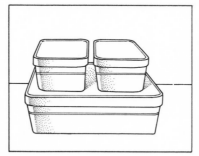
Stacking polythene boxes

tainers are easier to stack for storage in the freezer.

PACKING CASSEROLES FOR THE FREEZER
Turn on the 'rapid freeze' switch a couple of hours before required so that the freezer is very cold. For best results the food should be frozen as quickly as possible to prevent large ice crystals from forming in the food, which would then break down on thawing, causing loss of texture.

The food must also be completely cold before placing in the freezer. Pack the casserole into suitable containers and quantities for serving. The packs should not be too large as they would take a long time to freeze, thaw and reheat. It is better to have several smaller packages than one large one if cooking for large numbers. Large shallow containers are preferable as they freeze and reheat more quickly and are easier to stack in the freezer. If possible freeze the casserole in a container which can be reheated.

Pour the casserole into rigid freezing containers so that there is at least 1 cm ($\frac{1}{2}$ inch) headspace above the level of the food to allow for expansion when frozen (if filled right to the top, the frozen food will push off the lids and become prone to freezer burn). All solid food should be immersed in the liquid, but if it floats above the

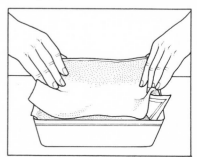
Weighting casserole with waxed paper

surface, weight it down with crumpled greaseproof or waxed paper. If container is only partly filled with food, use crumpled paper to fill up the space. As much air as possible should be excluded from polythene bags before sealing. All containers and bags should be well sealed to make them airtight. If in doubt, overwrap with polythene or foil.

Containers and bags should be

labelled with the type of casserole, number of servings and the date. Special freezer pens are available for marking.

It is also advisable to keep a record of all freezer entries with any comments about the recipe and how much seasoning or thickening, etc. was used. This enables you to know at a glance what is in the freezer, and ensures correct rotation of stock without any foods being stored longer than their recommended storage time.

PACKING THE FREEZER
Once the food is cold and securely wrapped it should be placed in the freezer as soon as possible. For initial freezing, place the packs in the coldest part of the freezer recommended by the manufacturer. This is usually the base and round the sides of a chest freezer, and on special freezing racks in an upright freezer. Space out the food to be frozen in the freezer and do not freeze too much at once: it is recommended not to freeze more than one-tenth of the freezer's capacity in any 24-hour period to ensure quick freezing of the food. Once the food is frozen solid it can be removed to another part of the freezer for storage, where packs can be stored tightly together with as little space between them as possible.

Return the switch to normal setting, and ensure that the door is properly sealed. A temperature of

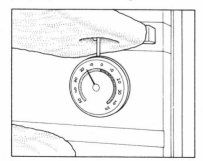

Freezer thermometer

−18°C (0°F) should be maintained for storing frozen food and a freezer thermometer is useful for

checking this. In an emergency such as a power cut do not be tempted to open the freezer until several hours after power has been restored (if no warm air is allowed in, the contents should remain frozen for 48 hours).

Storage times: For best results, casseroles should only be stored for 2 months in the freezer.

DEFROSTING
Casseroles may be defrosted slowly in the refrigerator, more quickly at room temperature, or quicker still by cooking straight from frozen (a microwave oven is also a successful way of defrosting and reheating quickly).

Defrost casseroles in their wrappings, but remove them if cooking straight from frozen and transfer to a casserole dish. Casseroles may be defrosted more quickly by tipping into a saucepan and heating gently and turning to prevent sticking. When they have defrosted sufficiently, they can be transferred to a casserole dish.

Defrosting and reheating times depend on the size and depth of the casserole. If reheating from frozen, place the casserole in a moderately hot oven for at least 1 hour until heated right through, then the temperature may be turned down for further cooking.

REHEATING CASSEROLES
The flavour and texture of casseroles is often improved by allowing them to cool and reheat 1 or 2 days later. This enables the many different ingredients to mix in the casserole and mellow the flavours so that the meat is really well penetrated with flavour.

Reheating is particularly beneficial for fatty meats as, on cooling, the fat will rise to the surface and may be spooned out or absorbed by kitchen paper or extracted with a bulb baster. If the casserole is chilled or frozen, the layer of fat on the surface will solidify so that it can easily be

Extracting fat with bulb baster

lifted off with a knife or spoon or spatula which ensures that all the fat is removed from the casserole.

Reheating casseroles is often convenient as preparation and cooking can be done in advance: 1 or 2 days if chilled or up to 2 months ahead if frozen. Reheat in a hot or cool oven, but always covered so that food does not dry out.

All reheated food should be thoroughly heated through and simmered for at least 10 minutes.

Reheating times depend on the type of food and size of dish. Delicate foods such as fish, fruit and vegetables will require less cooking than meat casseroles. Stir occasionally during reheating for even heating and a smooth sauce.

Spooning vegetables around meat

Once the casserole is thoroughly reheated it may be served straight from the dish. Large pieces of meat or joints may be arranged on a serving platter or dish and the sauce and vegetables spooned around and then garnished.

Vegetable and Fruit Casseroles

Fruits and vegetables, as well as being constituents of meat casseroles, make delicious casseroles in their own rights.

Vegetable casseroles can be served as starters, main course casseroles and vegetarian meals, and as vegetable accompaniments.

Fruit casseroles are served as a dessert and may be hot or cold.

VEGETABLES

Casseroles would be very dull without the wide variety of vegetables to add colour, texture, flavour and nutrients. Vegetable casseroles are also extremely versatile and may be served on numerous occasions: as a starter; main course or vegetarian casserole; as flavouring and 'stretching' of a meat casserole; or as a vegetable accompaniment. Vegetable casseroles are usually served hot but are sometimes cold as can be the case with ratatouille.

Some vegetables such as carrots, potatoes and onions, benefit from long, slow cooking in a casserole and these can be fried at the beginning or layered up as for an 'all in one' casserole. Other vegetables such as beans and courgettes are softer and do not need such long cooking and these can be added halfway through the cooking time. If you like to have some of the vegetables still crunchy then add them near the end of the cooking time.

With prolonged cooking in a casserole many vegetables cook down to a pulp which can form the basis of a sauce without adding other thickening agents like flour.

Cooked vegetables puréed for a sauce
Alternatively, the vegetables and liquid can be removed from the casserole and liquidised to a purée and poured back as a sauce.

Vegetables are also useful to braise or pot roast meat or fish in a casserole: the vegetables are fried and then the meat is placed on top of the vegetables in a casserole with some liquid and cooked covered in a moderately slow oven. This makes the meat very tender and juicy with the added flavour, colour and texture of the vegetables; and is a complete meal all in one pot.

Vegetables as an accompaniment to other dishes can also be cooked in a casserole in the oven at the same time as the main casserole. This is a good way of cooking vegetables as they cook in their own juices (or a very little water, stock, wine, butter, etc.) and all the goodness is retained. This is labour- as well as fuel-saving and ideal for entertaining as the vegetables cook themselves without supervision and they are less likely to be overcooked.

Sprigs of fresh herbs added to a casserole give a delicious flavour and aroma and also look attractive. The most common herbs to use are thyme, parsley, sage, rosemary, bay leaf and oregano. If fresh herbs are not available, substitute half the quantity of dried herbs as they will have a much stronger flavour.

BUYING
The abundance of fresh vegetables available throughout the year gives a very wide variety to choose from. Some vegetables are available all year whereas others are seasonal and may be home grown or imported. Choose vegetables which are in season and therefore at their best and cheapest, and of course only buy vegetables which are absolutely fresh. Alternatively, frozen or canned vegetables may be used, but these will cook more quickly and will not give so much flavour to the casserole.

TYPES OF VEGETABLES
Vegetables can be divided into several classifications, depending on how they grow:

BRASSICAS *(cabbage (green, white, red), spring greens, cauli-*

flower, broccoli and calabrese, spinach, Brussels sprouts): All these vegetables may be added to casseroles, either whole or chopped, divided into pieces or florets. Cabbage may be stuffed: either whole or individual leaves blanched, stuffed and rolled into parcels. Spinach is also a delicious addition to casseroles.

Cabbage is often used as a base to braise game and other meats. Red cabbage is ideal to cook in a casserole as it takes a long time to cook and soften.

MUSHROOMS AND FUNGI

(cultivated: button, cap, flat mushrooms; wild: cèpe, oyster, chanterelle, morel, blewit; truffle): Mushrooms are often added to casseroles for their flavour, shape and colour. Button mushrooms have the most delicate flavour and remain pale coloured on cooking and are therefore useful for adding to fish and poultry casseroles. The more open, darker mushrooms have much more flavour and are best added to dark meat and to game casseroles.

Dirty-looking mushrooms may be washed and scrubbed, otherwise it is best to wipe them with a damp cloth, and trim off the ends of the stalk if necessary. It is unnecessary to peel mushrooms. Small mushrooms may be left whole and larger mushrooms may be halved, quartered or sliced. They may be fried with other vegetables before the casserole is cooked, or alternatively added raw towards the end of the cooking

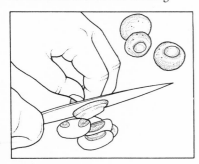

Slicing mushrooms

time. Dried mushrooms should be soaked in water before cooking, to soften them. Truffles may also be added to casseroles but are an extravagant luxury.

ONIONS *(brown, yellow, red and white skinned onions, shallots, pickling onions, spring onions, garlic; leeks)*: Almost every casserole includes onions in some form. They have a strong, pungent flavour which mellows with the long, slow cooking.

The outer skin is peeled off and small onions may be left whole. Larger onions may be cut into chunks, rings, dice or finely chopped. Garlic is very strong so one or two cloves, peeled and crushed, are usually enough to add to a casserole.

PODS AND SEEDS *(peas, mange-touts, beans (runner, French, broad), sweetcorn, okra)*: Whether shelled or cooked in their pods, peas and beans make colourful additions to casseroles. Peas and broad beans are usually shelled and added whole. Very young broad beans and mange-touts are cooked in their shells, either whole or chopped. Small French beans can be cooked whole while larger beans are sliced or cut into pieces.

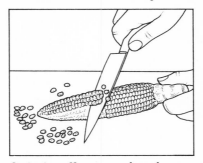

Stripping off sweetcorn kernels

Sweetcorn kernels are usually stripped off the cob for adding to casseroles. Okra is traditional in many African and creole casseroles and on cooking gives a characteristic 'sliminess' to the sauce. It may be left whole or sliced.

PULSES: These are the dried seeds of peas and beans and are extremely useful in casserole cooking for their high protein content and can therefore replace some or all of the meat. They include haricot, flageolet, butter bean, red kidney, black bean, black-eye pea, chick pea, soya, pinto, adzuki, split peas and lentils. Beans may also be sprouted, the most common being mung bean sprouts which are added to oriental casseroles. As they are dried, pulses make a useful store cupboard ingredient, but are best eaten within a year, after which they may become tough even after long cooking. Pulses all require long cooking to soften and are ideal for cooking in casseroles. They should also be soaked before cooking: either soak in cold water overnight, or pour over boiling water and soak for a couple of hours. After soaking they are usually simmered in water until tender which will take from half an hour to 2–3 hours, depending on the variety and age of the beans. The cooked beans can then be added to the casserole for further cooking and flavouring. Split peas and lentils can be added to casseroles without pre-soaking and cooking.

ROOTS *(carrot, swede, turnip, parsnip, beetroot, celeriac, salsify, kohlrabi)* and **TUBERS** *(potatoes, sweet potatoes, Jerusalem artichoke)*: Roots and tubers are often found in casseroles as they take longer to cook than most other vegetables. Most are at their best in the winter and are comparatively cheap.

The skins may be peeled or scrubbed and then left whole or cut up, depending on their size and the recipe used. They may be cut up into cubes, dice, slices (thick or thin) or julienne strips. Thinly sliced potatoes can often be used to cover a casserole such as hotpot.

SALAD LEAVES: Not often used in casserole cookery, but lettuce, chicory and Chinese cabbage may be added. Lettuce and chicory are delicious as a braised vegetable cooked in a casserole. Fish can also be wrapped in lettuce leaves before

Wrapping fish in lettuce leaves

cooking. Wild salad leaves such as sorrel and dandelion can also be added to casseroles.

STALKS *(celery, Florence fennel, chard, cardoons, seakale)* and **SHOOTS** *(asparagus, bamboo shoots, palm hearts, globe artichokes)*: Celery is the most popular of these vegetables for casseroles, as it is the most widely available and cheapest. It is usually cut into slices. Fennel is also now quite common and adds a distinctive aniseed flavour. Chard, cardoons and seakale stalks can be treated like celery and the leaves as for green, leafy vegetables.

Asparagus are a luxury for

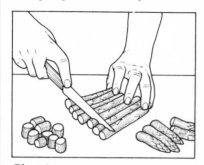

Chopping coarse asparagus stems

casseroles: the tips are usually re-served for garnishing the dish

while the coarser stems can be chopped and cooked with the casserole. Bamboo shoots and palm hearts are available in cans and add an oriental flavour to casseroles. Artichoke hearts are usually considered too good to add to casseroles, but whole artichokes may be stuffed and braised.

VEGETABLE FRUITS
(tomato, pepper, chilli, aubergine, avocado, olive, marrow, courgette, cucumber, pumpkin and squash): Tomato is the most popular of these vegetable fruits to use in casseroles, and together with peppers, aubergines, courgettes and olives add a Mediterranean flavour. Chillis are invaluable in many Asian and curried casseroles to add the characteristic 'hotness', and may be fresh, dried or ground powder. Most of these vegetables can also be halved and stuffed and baked in a casserole.

Tomatoes are usually skinned and the seeds removed before adding to casseroles: plunge into

Loosening tomato skins in hot water

boiling water for several seconds or until the skin peels away easily, then halve or quarter and scrape out the seeds. Peppers are usually cut into strips or rings and de-seeded. Aubergines are cooked with their skins on and cut into slices or cubes, and courgette and marrow are treated in the same way. (Aubergines should also be sprinkled with salt after preparing to draw out the juices which can be bitter.) Avocados are unusual in casseroles but are common in Mexican and South American

recipes. Pumpkin and squash are popular in North American casseroles, peeled and cut into cubes, or left whole and stuffed.

PREPARATION
Vegetables should be prepared carefully to ensure that they retain as much of their goodness as possible. So often, the tastiest and most nutritious parts of the vegetables are thrown away. The most obvious example of this wastage is with peeling potatoes and root vegetables as most of the nutrients are concentrated just below the skin and peeling them removes a high proportion of the goodness.

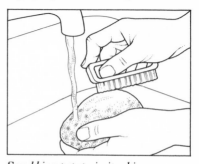

Scrubbing potato in its skin

Instead of peeling they can be well washed and scrubbed. Many other vegetables are also trimmed un-necessarily as only any damaged bits and roots and tough ends should be removed. For instance, the stalks of green vegetables can be chopped and cooked with the leaves; the green tops of leeks are just as good as the white stems; and the leaves from a cauliflower can be cooked as well as the head.

Ideally, vegetables should be prepared just before cooking, but if it is more convenient to prepare them in advance they may be covered and kept in the refriger-ator until required. Root vege-tables that have been peeled or cut up can be immersed in cold water to prevent them browning. For casseroles it is usual to cut up the vegetables, although small ones can be left whole. Wash and dry the vegetables before cutting on a chopping board with a sharp knife. They may be cut into halves, quarters, wedges, large cubes, dice, thick or thin slices, shreds, julienne strips, or finely chopped. The smaller the vegetables are cut, the quicker they will cook in the casserole, so if you prefer the vegetables slightly crisp cut them into large pieces.

Vegetables can also be used as a garnish for casseroles, for example

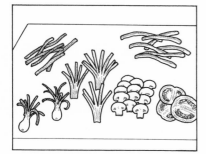

Garnishes for casseroles

thinly sliced red or green peppers; sticks of celery or spring onions cut into 'curled brushes'; slices of tomato or mushrooms; and of course sprigs of fresh herbs.

STORAGE
Vegetables should be used as soon as possible after they are picked to preserve their flavour and nutrients. If they must be stored, keep them in a cool airy place such as a larder or cover and store in the refrigerator.

For longer storage vegetables may be frozen and stored in the freezer (vegetables must be blanched in boiling water before freezing to destroy the enzymes which would otherwise deteriorate the vegetables). Frozen vegetables may be added to a casserole while still frozen or may be thawed first.

FRUIT

Fruit can be used in casserole cookery as an addition to meat and vegetable casseroles, or as a fruit casserole served either hot or cold as a dessert such as fruit compote.

Fruit is used in savoury dishes to add sweetness, sharpness and a contrasting colour and texture. Acidic fruits are often added to fatty foods to counteract their richness, as, for example, in duck cooked in orange. Fruit may be added in the form of juice, whole small fruits or sliced or chopped fruit. It may be used to stuff meat, be part of the sauce or form an attractive garnish.

Fruit casseroles are an ideal way to prepare fruits that need cooking. Fruits are cooked to make them tender with added flavourings such as sweeteners and spices. If this cooking is done in a casserole the fruit can cook in its own juices or a minimum of flavourings, such as fruit juice or wine, and the fruit will remain in whole pieces.

TYPES OF FRUIT AND NUTS

APPLES AND PEARS (*variety of dessert and cooking apples and pears*): Both the sweet and sour cooking apples can be used in sweet and savoury casseroles. They may be cooked whole with their peel on; or may be peeled, cored and sliced or chopped.

BERRIES AND CURRANTS (*strawberries, raspberries, blackberries, gooseberries, cranberries, black, red and white currants*): These soft fruits are usually used for sweet casseroles, either on their own or as a mixture with other fruits. However, gooseberries are traditionally cooked with mackerel, and cranberries with turkey, and the Scots sometimes stuff grouse and other game birds with raspberries.

CITRUS FRUITS (*orange, lemon, lime, grapefruit, tangerine*):

Citrus fruits can be added to sweet and savoury casseroles in a variety of ways: the rind can be grated or

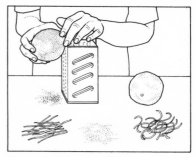

Preparing citrus rind

cut into long shreds; the flesh cut into segments or slices; and the juice squeezed out.

STONE FRUITS (*cherries, plums, peaches, apricots*): These add a rich colour and flavour to sweet and savoury casseroles. Small fruits can be cooked whole and may be stoned. Larger fruits

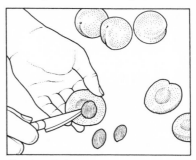

Stoning fruit

are usually halved and stoned, and sometimes cut into slices.

TROPICAL FRUITS (*banana, pineapple, mango, papaya, guava, pomegranate, fig, dates*): These give an exotic flavour to sweet and savoury casseroles. Pineapple pieces are often used for 'sweet and sour' casseroles, and papaya is extremely useful for tenderising tough meat as it contains an enzyme which breaks down the protein. These fruits are usually peeled and then cut into slices or chunks.

VINE FRUITS (*grapes, melons*):
Green grapes are often added to
fish and poultry casseroles and
termed 'Véronique': grapes can be
cooked whole or halved and

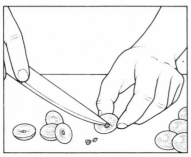

Seeding grapes

seeded and can also be added to
sweet casseroles.

DRIED FRUITS (*sultanas,
raisins, apricots, apples, dates,
prunes, figs, pears etc.*): Dried
fruits are very useful to keep in the
store cupboard to add to sweet and
savoury casseroles. The long, slow
cooking is ideal to soften them.
For savoury casseroles they may
be added to the sauce or stuffings
and may be left whole or chopped.

NUTS (*peanuts, cashews, walnuts,
almond, hazelnuts, brazil, chestnuts,
pine nuts, pistachio, coconut*):
There are numerous nuts which
can be added to sweet and savoury
casseroles. The nuts must be
shelled but may be used with or
without the thin inside skin. They
may be used whole, chopped or
ground, for stuffings or sauces or
just sprinkled into a casserole.
They also make attractive
garnishes. Grated coconut is often
added to curried casseroles.
    Nuts are also high in protein
and therefore valuable for adding
to vegetarian casseroles.

STORAGE
Fresh fruit is very perishable, and
should be used as soon as possible,
and this is particularly important
with soft fruits. They should be
stored in a cool, airy place, or
covered in the refrigerator. For
longer storage of 6–12 months,
fruits may be frozen, either whole
or after preparation.
    Commerically frozen fruits may
also be used for casseroles and
stored in the freezer (these will
produce a considerable amount of
juice on thawing and this can also
be added to the casserole).
    Canned fruits can be stored in a
cupboard for longer storage, and
the syrup or juice may also be
added to the casserole.
    Dried fruits may be stored in
airtight containers for up to
one year.

PREPARATION
Fruits should be washed and
dried, and then prepared according to the type of fruit and individual recipes. Stalks and leaves
should be removed, then the fruit
may be left whole, or peeled,
stoned, cut into slices, chopped or
grated. Alternatively, the fruit
may be squeezed to a juice or
blended to a purée.
    Firm fruits such as apples and
dried fruit may be added at the
beginning of cooking, whereas
softer fruits such as banana and
grapes may be added towards the
end of the cooking time.
    Fruits for sweet casseroles are
prepared in the same way and
placed in a casserole dish with
flavourings such as sugar, spices
and a little liquid (fruit juice,
wine, water) or may be cooked in
their own juices. The fruit is
cooked gently until tender and the
juice may be thickened with cornflour or arrowroot. Fruit
casseroles may be served either
hot or cold.

VEGETABLE AND FRUIT CASSEROLES

Serve vegetable casseroles with
grilled or roast meat. Fruit casseroles make an unusual dessert,
and can be popped in the oven at
the same time as a main dish.

CABBAGE AND TOMATO CASSEROLE

Serves 4

15 ml (1 tbsp) vegetable oil
25 g (1 oz) butter
2 medium onions, skinned and sliced
1 garlic clove, skinned and crushed
3 tomatoes, skinned and quartered
15 ml (1 tbsp) plain flour
300 ml ($\frac{1}{2}$ pint) chicken stock
salt and freshly ground pepper
5 ml (1 tsp) sugar
450 g (1 lb) white cabbage, trimmed
60 ml (4 tbsp) natural yogurt

1 Heat the oil and butter in a
large pan, add the onions and
garlic and cook for 5 minutes until
they are soft.

2 Add the tomatoes and continue cooking for 2 minutes.
Stir in the flour and continue
cooking, stirring continuously.

3 Remove the pan from the heat
and gradually add the stock.
Bring to the boil, stirring. Add
seasoning and sugar.

4 Place the cabbage in a 1.1 litre
(2 pint) casserole and pour
over the tomato mixture.

5 Cover and cook in the oven at
170°C (325°F) mark 3 for $1\frac{1}{2}$
hours until tender.

6 Stir the yogurt into the casserole 10 minutes before the
end of the cooking time.

BAKED PARSNIPS IN ORANGE

Serves 4

450 g (1 lb) parsnips, peeled

150 ml (¼ pint) unsweetened orange juice

50 g (2 oz) butter

salt and freshly ground pepper

15 ml (1 tbsp) demerara sugar

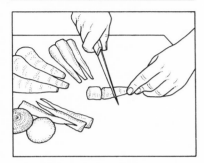

1 Cut the parsnips into bite-sized pieces, removing the woody core if they are old and large.

2 Place the parsnips and orange juice in a pan, bring to the boil and simmer gently for 5 minutes.

3 Turn into a greased casserole, dot with butter, season and sprinkle with the sugar.

4 Cover and cook in the oven at 190°C (375°F) mark 5 for 1 hour until tender.

ANNA POTATOES

Serves 4

700 g (1½ lb) even-sized waxy potatoes, peeled

salt and freshly ground pepper

50–75 g (2–3 oz) butter, melted

chopped fresh parsley, to garnish

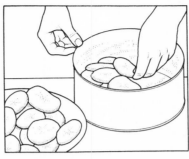

1 Grease a round cake tin and line the base with grease-proof paper. Slice the potatoes thinly and arrange in layers, over-lapping the slices.

2 Sprinkle each layer with seasoning and spoon over melted butter. Continue until potatoes are used.

3 Press down well, cover with greaseproof paper or foil and cook in the oven at 190°C (375°F) mark 5 for about 1 hour, until the top is golden brown. Add more butter during the cooking time if the potato looks dry.

4 Turn out, cut into wedges and sprinkle surface with chopped fresh parsley.

BEAN AND VEGETABLE STEW

Serves 4

175 g (6 oz) cannellini beans, soaked overnight in cold water

750 ml (1¼ pints) chicken stock

salt and freshly ground pepper

25 g (1 oz) butter

225 g (8 oz) courgettes, trimmed and sliced

3 celery stalks, trimmed and sliced

1 medium onion, skinned and sliced

1 small red pepper, seeded and sliced

225 g (8 oz) aubergine, diced

150 ml (¼ pint) dry cider

10 ml (2 tsp) chopped fresh thyme

1 Drain the beans and place in a flameproof casserole with the stock and seasoning. Bring to the boil, cover and simmer for 1 hour, until the beans are tender but still firm.

2 Melt the butter in a large deep frying pan and sauté the courgettes, celery, onion, pepper and aubergine, a few at a time, for 5–10 minutes until golden.

3 Add the vegetables to the beans and stock. Add the cider and thyme, cover and simmer gently for 30 minutes, until the beans and vegetables are tender.

RATATOUILLE

Serves 4

30 ml (2 tbsp) vegetable oil

25 g (1 oz) butter

4 tomatoes, skinned and sliced

2 aubergines, sliced

1 small green pepper, seeded and sliced

2 onions, skinned and sliced

2 courgettes, sliced

salt and freshly ground pepper

1 garlic clove, skinned and crushed

1 Heat the oil and butter in a flameproof casserole and add the prepared vegetables, seasoning and garlic.

2 Stir well, cover tightly and cook in the oven at 180°C (350°F) mark 4 for 1–1½ hours, until the vegetables are tender.

VEGETABLE POT

Serves 4

40 g (1½ oz) butter or margarine

1 onion, skinned and sliced

3 courgettes, trimmed and sliced

1 small green pepper, seeded and sliced

1 garlic clove, skinned and crushed

2.5 ml (½ tsp) ground coriander

2.5 ml (½ tsp) ground cumin

40 g (1½ oz) plain flour

600 ml (1 pint) vegetable stock

salt and freshly ground pepper

4 tomatoes, skinned

175 g (6 oz) haricot beans, soaked overnight then cooked

30 ml (2 tbsp) tomato purée

1 Melt the butter or margarine in a flameproof casserole and add the vegetables and spices. Fry for about 15 minutes until the vegetables are soft.

2 Stir in the flour and cook for 2 minutes. Gradually stir in the stock and bring to the boil to thicken, then season well.

3 Roughly chop the tomatoes and stir into the pan with the beans and tomato purée.

4 Cover and simmer gently for 35 minutes, until all the vegetables are tender.

OVEN-COOKED RICE

Serves 4

225 g (8 oz) long-grain rice

600 ml (1 pint) water

5 ml (1 tsp) salt

1 Place the rice in a casserole. Bring the water and salt to the boil, pour over the rice and stir the mixture well.

2 Cover tightly and bake in the oven at 180°C (350°F) mark 4 for 35–40 minutes, or until the grains are just soft and the cooking liquid has all been absorbed by the rice.

——— VARIATIONS ———

Although rice is most usually cooked in water, it can also be cooked in other liquids to give extra flavour and variety. The water may be replaced by any of the following:
Chicken or beef stock (fresh or made from a cube).
Canned tomato juice, undiluted or used half-and-half with water.
Orange juice—used half-and-half with water.

ALMOND-STUFFED APPLES

Serves 8

8 large cooking apples, cored

100 g (4 oz) marzipan

8 walnut halves

50 g (2 oz) butter, melted

pouring cream, to serve

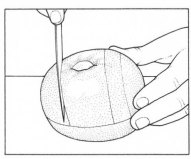

1 With a pointed knife, make a slit around the middle circumference of each apple. On the top half make 5 to 6 slits down to the middle. Place the apples in a roasting tin.

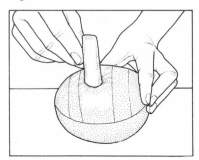

2 Cut the marzipan into eight long sticks and insert one into each core cavity. Top with a walnut half. Brush all over with melted butter and cover with foil.

3 Bake in the oven at 240°C (450°F) mark 8 for 25 minutes.

4 Lower the temperature to 180°C (350°F) mark 4, remove the foil and cook for 30–40 minutes or until soft but not floppy. Serve with pouring cream.

CINNAMON APRICOTS IN CREAM

Serves 4

450 g (1 lb) apricots, halved and stoned

75 ml (5 tbsp) water

65 g (2½ oz) sugar

2.5 ml (½ tsp) ground cinnamon

45 ml (3 tbsp) double cream

1 Place the apricots in an oven-proof dish. Mix the water, sugar and cinnamon and pour over the apricots.

2 Cover and bake in the oven at 190°C (375°F) mark 5 for 25–30 minutes, until the apricots are just tender.

3 Pour cream over and bake for 10 minutes more.

BANANAS IN ORANGE

Serves 4

grated rind and juice of 1 orange

25 g (1 oz) butter or margarine

30 ml (2 tbsp) maple syrup

50 g (2 oz) seedless raisins

4 bananas

1 Put the orange rind and juice, fat and maple syrup into a saucepan and heat gently until the fat has melted. Stir in the raisins and remove from the heat.

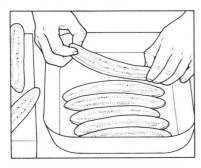

2 Peel and cut the bananas in half lengthways. Lay them side by side in a shallow ovenproof dish. Pour over the hot syrup and cover with foil.

3 Bake in the oven at 190°C (375°F) mark 5 for about 20 minutes, or until the bananas are just tender. Serve hot with soured cream, if liked.

BUTTERY PEACHES

Serves 6

6 peaches, peeled, halved and stoned

225 ml (8 fl oz) water

100 g (4 oz) sugar

30 ml (2 tbsp) lemon juice

25 g (1 oz) butter

1 Place the peaches in an oven-proof dish. Put the water, sugar, lemon juice and butter into a saucepan. Bring to the boil; simmer for 5 minutes. Pour the syrup over the peaches. Cover and bake in the oven at 170°C (325°F) mark 3 for 30 minutes, or until the peaches are tender but still hold their shape.

BAKED FRUIT FLAMBÉ

Serves 8

1 small fresh pineapple

60 ml (4 tbsp) thick honey

2.5 ml (½ tsp) ground cinnamon

50 g (2 oz) butter

150 ml (¼ pint) water

4 oranges, peeled and segmented

350 g (12 oz) fresh apricots, halved and stoned

60 ml (4 tbsp) rum or vodka

pouring cream, to serve

1 Trim off both ends of the pineapple, then cut it into 1 cm (½ inch) slices.

2 Remove the skin with a sharp knife and the centre core with an apple corer. Cut the rings into 6–8 segments each.

3 Heat the honey, cinnamon, butter and water until well mixed. Arrange all the fruit in a shallow ovenproof dish and pour over the honey mixture.

4 Cover and bake in the oven at 180°C (350°F) mark 4 for 50 minutes, until the apricots are tender. Transfer to a pre-heated chafing dish, placed over a lighted burner.

5 Heat the rum or vodka in a small pan. Pour it over the fruit, set alight and serve immediately, flaming. Serve with thick pouring cream.

TIPSY FRUIT COMPOTE

Serves 8

275 g (10 oz) dried prunes, soaked overnight

275 g (10 oz) dried apricots, soaked overnight

50 g (2 oz) sultanas, soaked overnight

75 g (3 oz) dried apple rings, soaked overnight

1 cinnamon stick

60 ml (4 tbsp) whisky

600 ml (1 pint) unsweetened orange juice

15 ml (1 tbsp) soft brown sugar

pared rind of 1 lemon

3 bananas

1 Drain the soaked fruit and place in an ovenproof dish with the cinnamon stick.

2 Combine the whisky, orange juice and sugar and pour over fruit. Thinly shred the lemon rind and scatter over.

3 Cover with foil and bake at 180°C (350°F) mark 4 for about 30 minutes.

4 Leave to cool. Slice the bananas and add before serving the compote.

Basic Recipes

Stocks, toppings and accompaniments, marinades and flavourings all play an important part in helping you to create the tastiest of casseroles.

STOCKS

Stocks play almost as important a part in flavouring casseroles as they do in soups. Choose the appropriate stock for each type of meat, whether beef, lamb, veal or chicken. For vegetable casseroles, you can use any of the meat stocks you prefer.

WHITE STOCK

Makes about 1.7 litres (3 pints)

900 g (2 lb) knuckle of veal, chopped
2.3 litres (4 pints) water
little lemon juice
1 onion, skinned and sliced
2 carrots, sliced
bouquet garni
5 ml (1 tsp) salt

1 Put the bones in a large pan, add the water and lemon juice, bring to the boil and remove any scum that rises.

2 Add the vegetables, bouquet garni and salt, reboil, cover and simmer for 5–6 hours.

3 Strain the stock thoroughly and leave to cool. When cold remove any fat.

FISH STOCK

Makes about 300 ml ($\frac{1}{2}$ pint)

1 fish head or fish bones and trimmings
450 ml ($\frac{3}{4}$ pint) water
salt
bouquet garni
1 onion, skinned and sliced

1 Clean the head or wash the fish trimmings. Put in a saucepan, cover with water, add some salt, bring to the boil and skim.

2 Reduce the heat and add the bouquet garni and onion. Cover, simmer for 20 minutes and strain thoroughly.

3 Use on the same day, or store in the refrigerator for not more than 2 days.

CHICKEN STOCK

Makes 1.1–1.4 litres (2–2$\frac{1}{2}$ pints)

carcass and bones of a cooked chicken
1.4–1.7 litres (2$\frac{1}{2}$–3 pints) water
1 onion, skinned and sliced
1 carrot, peeled and sliced
1 celery stalk, trimmed and sliced
bouquet garni (optional)

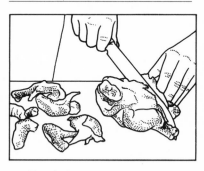

1 Break down the carcass and bones of the cooked chicken, and make sure to include any skin and chicken scraps.

2 Put in a pan with the water, onion, carrot, celery and the bouquet garni, if using.

3 Bring to the boil, skim and simmer, covered, for about 3 hours.

4 Strain the stock thoroughly, discarding the flavouring vegetables, and leave to cool. When cold, remove all traces of fat.

BEEF STOCK
Makes about 1.4 litres (2½ pints)

450 g (1 lb) shin of beef, cut into pieces

450 g (1 lb) marrowbone or knuckle of veal, chopped

1.7 litres (3 pints) water

bouquet garni

1 onion, skinned and sliced

1 carrot, peeled and sliced

1 celery stalk, trimmed and sliced

salt

1 To give a good flavour and colour, brown the bones and meat in the oven (exact temperature not important) before using.

2 Put in a pan with the water, bouquet garni, vegetables and salt. Bring to the boil, skim and simmer, covered, for 5–6 hours.

3 Strain the stock thoroughly, discarding the vegetables, and leave until cool. Remove fat.

VEGETABLE STOCK
A tasty stock can be made from vegetables alone. Choose fresh vegetables such as outer leaves of cabbage or other green vegetables, peelings from root vegetables such as carrots, parsnips and potatoes, and leek trimmings. A few bacon rinds can be added for extra flavour. Chop the vegetables if necessary, put into a pan and cover with cold water. Add a few peppercorns, cover and simmer for about 30 minutes, then strain. Use as soon as possible.

MARINADES AND FLAVOURINGS

A marinade adds not only flavour to a casserole, but also helps to tenderise the meat. Choose from any of the recipes here and leave the prepared meat in it to marinate overnight. Drain, fry the meat and any vegetables, tip in the marinade and cook as usual. The casserole may be further enhanced by the addition of a bouquet garni or other flavouring.

MARINADES

LIME MARINADE FOR CHICKEN

100 ml (4 fl oz) lime juice

45 ml (3 tbsp) vegetable oil

15 ml (1 tbsp) grated lime rind

20 ml (4 tsp) salt

1.25 ml (¼ tsp) crushed peppercorns

1 Mix the lime juice with the vegetable oil, then stir in the remaining ingredients.

SPRING ONION AND SOY MARINADE FOR CHICKEN

100 ml (4 fl oz) soy sauce

30 ml (2 tbsp) dry sherry

50 g (2 oz) spring onions, thinly sliced

30 ml (2 tbsp) soft light brown sugar

2.5 ml (½ tsp) salt

2.5 ml (½ tsp) ground ginger

1 Mix the soy sauce with the dry sherry, then stir in the remaining ingredients.

ORANGE HERB MARINADE FOR CHICKEN

150 ml (¼ pint) white wine or dry vermouth

45 ml (3 tbsp) olive oil

juice of 2 oranges

5 ml (1 tsp) each of chopped fresh rosemary, thyme and marjoram

1 garlic clove, skinned and crushed

1 Mix the white wine or vermouth with the olive oil. Stir in the remaining ingredients.

MARINADE FOR LAMB

75 ml (3 fl oz) red wine

60 ml (4 tbsp) olive oil

5 ml (1 tsp) chopped fresh thyme or 2.5 ml (½ tsp) dried

2.5 ml (½ tsp) ground cumin

5 ml (1 tsp) chopped fresh marjoram or 2.5 ml (½ tsp) dried

5 ml (1 tsp) salt

1 garlic clove, skinned and crushed

5 ml (1 tsp) lemon or lime juice

1 Mix together the red wine and olive oil. Stir in the remaining ingredients.

MARINADE FOR VENISON

2 carrots, peeled and chopped

2 small onions, skinned and chopped

1 celery stalk, trimmed and chopped

6 peppercorns

parsley stalks

bay leaf

3 blades of mace

red wine

1 Place the vegetables and flavourings in a large container, put in the venison and add wine to half-cover it. Marinate for 12 hours, turning occasionally.

2 Remove the meat and cook as desired. Boil the marinade to reduce; strain, and use for gravy.

MARINADE FOR PORK

150 ml (¼ pint) dry white wine

45 ml (3 tbsp) vinegar

4 cloves garlic, skinned and crushed

1.25 ml (¼ tsp) ground cloves

2.5 ml (½ tsp) dried marjoram

freshly ground pepper

1 Mix together the wine and the vinegar, then stir in the garlic and seasonings.

BOUQUET GARNI
(USING DRIED HERBS)

1 small bay leaf

pinch of dried mixed herbs

6 peppercorns

pinch of dried parsley

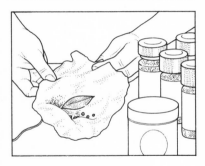

1 Tie the herbs together in a small square of muslin with string or cotton, leaving a long end free to tie the bouquet garni to the handle of the pan.

TRADITIONAL BOUQUET GARNI

1 bay leaf

1 sprig of parsley

1 sprig of thyme

few peppercorns

1 Tie in a small piece of muslin. You can, of course, choose some other fresh herbs.

TOPPINGS AND ACCOMPANIMENTS

A crisp, crunchy topping makes the perfect foil for the melting texture of casseroles. Almost any sort of pastry can be used as a topping when reheating casseroles in a pie dish. Choose dumplings for a more substantial addition. Accompaniments such as garlic bread make a change from the usual vegetables.

PUFF PASTRY

450 g (1 lb) strong plain flour

pinch of salt

450 g (1 lb) butter

300 ml (½ pint) iced water

15 ml (1 tbsp) lemon juice

beaten egg, to glaze

1 Mix the flour and salt together in a bowl. Cut off 50 g (2 oz) of butter and pat the remaining butter with a rolling pin to a slab 2 cm (¾ inch) thick.

2 Rub the 50 g (2 oz) of butter into the flour. Stir in enough water and lemon juice to make a soft, elastic dough. Knead dough until smooth, shape into a round.

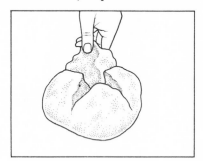

3 Cut through half the depth in the shape of a cross. Open out the flaps to form a star. Roll out, keeping the centre four times as thick as the flaps.

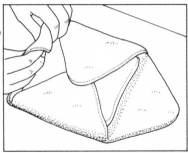

4 Place the slab of butter in the centre of the dough and fold over the flaps, envelope-style. Press gently with a rolling pin and roll out into a rectangle measuring about 40 × 20 cm (16 × 8 inches).

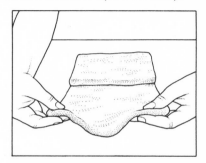

5 Fold the bottom third up and the top third down, keeping the edges straight. Seal the edges by pressing with the rolling pin.

6 Wrap the pastry in greaseproof paper and leave in the refrigerator to 'rest' for 30 minutes.

7 Put the pastry on a lightly floured working surface with the folded edges to the sides and repeat the rolling, folding and resting sequence five times.

8 After the final resting, roll out the pastry on a lightly floured surface and shape as required. Brush with beaten egg before baking. The usual oven temperature is 230°C (450°F) mark 8.

SHORTCRUST PASTRY

225 g (8 oz) plain flour

pinch of salt

50 g (2 oz) butter or block margarine

50 g (2 oz) lard

30–45 ml (2–3 tbsp) chilled water

1 Sift the flour and salt together in a bowl. Cut the butter or margarine and lard into small pieces and add to the flour.

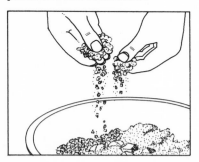

2 Lightly rub in the butter or margarine and the lard, using fingertips, until the mixture resembles fine breadcrumbs.

3 Add the chilled water evenly over the surface and stir in until the mixture begins to stick together in large lumps.

4 With one hand, collect the mixture together to form a ball. Knead lightly for a few seconds to give a firm, smooth dough. Do not over-handle.

5 The pastry can be used straight away, but it is better if allowed to 'rest' for about 30 minutes wrapped in foil and placed in the refrigerator.

6 Roll out the pastry on a lightly floured surface to a thickness of 3 mm ($\frac{1}{8}$ inch). Do not pull or stretch the pastry. To cook, the usual oven temperature is 200–220°C (400–425°F) mark 6–7.

SUETCRUST PASTRY

225 g (8 oz) self-raising flour

salt

100 g (4 oz) shredded suet

about 150 ml ($\frac{1}{4}$ pint) cold water

1 Mix the flour, salt and suet together in a bowl. Stir in enough cold water to give a light, elastic dough. Knead very gently until smooth.

2 Roll or pat out on a lightly floured surface to 2.5 cm (1 inch) thick. Place carefully on top of a casserole 20–25 minutes before the end of the cooking time.

3 Simmer on top of the cooker or bake in the oven at 200°C (400°F) mark 6 unless otherwise stated in the recipe.

ROUGH PUFF PASTRY

225 g (8 oz) plain flour

pinch of salt

75 g (3 oz) butter or block margarine

75 g (3 oz) lard

about 150 ml ($\frac{1}{4}$ pint) cold water and a squeeze of lemon juice

beaten egg, to glaze

1 Mix the flour and salt together in a bowl. Cut the fat (which should be quite firm) into cubes about 2 cm ($\frac{3}{4}$ inch) across.

2 Stir the fat into the flour without breaking up the pieces. Add enough water and lemon juice to mix to a fairly stiff dough.

3 On a lightly floured surface, roll out into an oblong three times as long as it is wide. Fold the bottom third up and the top third down, then turn the pastry so that folded edges are at the sides.

4 Seal the ends of the pastry by pressing them lightly with a rolling pin.

5 Repeat this rolling and folding process three more times, turning the dough so that the folded edge is on the left hand side each time.

6 Wrap the pastry in greaseproof paper and leave to 'rest' in the refrigerator or a cool place for about 30 minutes before using.

7 Roll out the pastry on a lightly floured surface to 3 mm ($\frac{1}{8}$ inch) thick and use as required. Brush with beaten egg before baking. The usual oven temperature is 220°C (425°F) mark 7.

CHOUX PASTRY

Serves 4

50 g (2 oz) butter or block margarine
150 ml (¼ pint) water
65 g (2½ oz) plain flour, sifted
2 eggs, lightly beaten (see method)
15 ml (1 tbsp) chopped fresh parsley

1 Put the fat and water together in a saucepan, heat gently until the fat has melted, then bring to the boil. Remove the pan from the heat.

2 Tip all the flour at once into the hot liquid. Beat thoroughly with a wooden spoon, then return the pan to the heat.

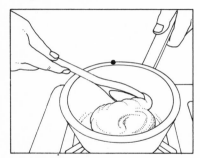

3 Continue beating the mixture until it is smooth and forms a ball in the centre of the pan. (Take care not to over-beat or the mixture will become fatty.)

4 Remove from the heat and leave the mixture to cool for a minute or two.

5 Beat in the eggs a little at a time, adding only just enough to give a piping consistency. (Use size 4 eggs if beating by hand and size 2 eggs when using an electric mixer for beating.)

6 It is important to beat the mixture vigorously at this stage to trap in as much air as possible until the mixture develops a sheen.

7 Beat in the parsley. Spoon or pipe the mixture around the edge of a casserole about 45 minutes before the end of the cooking time. Bake in the oven, uncovered, at 200°C (400°F) mark 6 until choux is risen and golden brown.

PASTRY PUFFS

225 g (8 oz) puff pastry (see page 154)
beaten egg, to glaze

1 Thinly roll out the pastry on a lightly floured surface. Stamp out different-sized fluted rounds and make a small hole in the centre of each.

2 Transfer to a dampened baking sheet, brush with beaten egg and bake in the oven at 220°C (425°F) mark 7 for about 15 minutes until golden brown and risen. Scatter the pastry rounds over a casserole.

POTATO DUMPLINGS

Serves 6

1.4 kg (3 lb) potatoes, peeled
5 ml (1 tsp) salt
2.5 ml (½ tsp) grated nutmeg
50 g (2 oz) semolina
75 g (3 oz) wheatmeal flour
2 eggs, beaten
2 slices of bread
butter

1 Cook and sieve the potatoes and leave to become cold. Add the salt, nutmeg, semolina, flour and eggs and knead until a smooth dough is formed.

2 Cut the bread into small dice and fry until light brown in hot butter.

3 Flour the hands, make round dumplings about the size of a fist with the dough and press a few of the fried croûtons into each.

4 Put the dumplings into boiling salted water and cook them for about 12–15 minutes.

5 Place them on a flat dish and pour melted butter over the top. Serve with a casserole.

FORCEMEAT BALLS
Makes 6

125 g (4 oz) streaky bacon, rinded and finely chopped

1 small onion, skinned and finely chopped

25 g (1 oz) butter, margarine or shredded suet

125 g (4 oz) fresh breadcrumbs

30 ml (2 tbsp) chopped fresh herbs or 10 ml (2 tsp) dried herbs

salt and freshly ground pepper

1 egg, beaten

1 Fry the bacon in its own fat until soft. Add the onion and fry until golden.

2 Turn into a bowl and beat in the fat. Stir in the breadcrumbs, herbs and seasoning.

3 Bind the mixture with the beaten egg and shape into six even-sized balls.

4 Place the balls between the meat in a casserole, cover and cook in the oven at 190°C (375°F) mark 5 for 30 minutes.

SWIMMERS
Makes 8

125 g (4 oz) strong plain flour

2.5 ml (½ tsp) salt

15 g (½ oz) fresh yeast or 5 ml (1 tsp) dried yeast and 2.5 ml (½ tsp) sugar

75 ml (3 fl oz) warm water

1 Sift the flour and salt into a bowl. If using fresh yeast, blend with the water or if using dried yeast, add it with the sugar to the warm water and leave in a warm place for about 15 minutes until frothy.

2 Make a well in the centre of the bowl and add the yeast liquid. Mix the dough until it leaves the sides of the bowl. Turn on to a floured surface and knead well for 10 minutes until elastic.

3 Place in a bowl and cover with a clean cloth. Leave to rise in a warm place for about 1 hour until doubled in size.

4 Divide the risen dough into eight pieces and gently form into balls. Place on the top of the casserole ingredients about 30 minutes before the cooking time is complete.

5 Cover the casserole again and simmer gently on top of the cooker or bake in the oven at 200°C (400°F) mark 6 until the swimmers swell and are cooked right through.

DUMPLINGS
Makes 8

100 g (4 oz) suetcrust pastry (see page 155)

freshly chopped or dried herbs (optional)

salt and freshly ground pepper

1 Make the pastry, adding herbs and seasoning to the dry mix. Divide the pastry into eight equal pieces and shape into balls.

2 Add the dumplings to a casserole about 15–25 minutes before cooking is complete, then reduce the heat and cover the casserole again.

3 Simmer gently on top of the cooker or bake in the oven at 200°C (400°F) mark 6, unless otherwise stated, until the dumplings swell. Do not allow the liquid to boil or the dumplings will disintegrate.

SAVOURY CRUMBLE

175 g (6 oz) plain flour

75 g (3 oz) butter or block margarine

5 ml (1 tsp) chopped fresh herbs or 2.5 ml (½ tsp) dried herbs

salt and freshly ground pepper

1 Place the flour in a bowl and rub in the fat until the mixture resembles fine breadcrumbs. Stir in the herbs and seasoning.

2 Sprinkle the mixture on top of a casserole and bake in the oven at 400°C (200°F) mark 6 for about 30 minutes until golden.

BACON THATCH

125 g (4 oz) wide streaky bacon, rinded

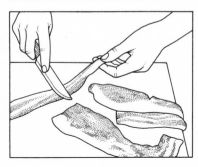

1 On a wooden board, stretch each rasher of bacon using the back of a knife and divide into two pieces.

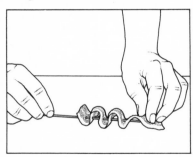

2 Concertina the bacon by threading on to skewers. Place the skewers on a flat tin and bake alongside casserole until crisp. Arrange over the top of a casserole.

SWEDE AND POTATO LATTICE

350 g (12 oz) potato, peeled
350 g (12 oz) swede, peeled
25 g (1 oz) butter or margarine
salt and freshly ground pepper
25 g (1 oz) Cheddar cheese, grated

1 Cook the potato and swede in salted water until tender. Drain very well, push through a mouli or wire sieve.

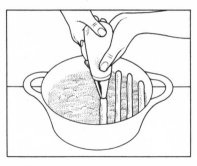

2 Beat in the fat, then season. Pipe or spoon over a casserole, sprinkle the cheese on top and flash under the grill to brown.

COBBLERS

Makes about 12

225 g (8 oz) self-raising flour
1.25 ml ($\frac{1}{4}$ tsp) salt
50 g (2 oz) butter or block margarine
30 ml (2 tbsp) chopped fresh parsley (optional)
about 150 ml ($\frac{1}{4}$ pint) milk

1 Place the flour and salt into a bowl. Rub in the fat until the mixture resembles fine bread-crumbs. Add the parsley if using.

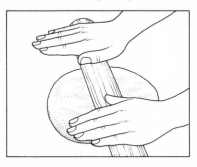

2 Make a well in the centre and add sufficient milk to give a soft but manageable dough. Turn out on to a lightly floured surface, knead lightly and roll out the dough to 1 cm ($\frac{1}{2}$ inch) thickness.

3 Cut out rounds using a 4 cm (1$\frac{1}{2}$ inch) plain cutter. Brush with milk and arrange overlapping around the edge of the casserole.

4 Bake in the oven at 220°C (425°F) mark 7 for 10–15 minutes until the topping is golden brown.

GARLIC BREAD

100 g (4 oz) butter
2 garlic cloves, skinned
salt and freshly ground pepper
1 French loaf

1 Soften the butter and beat until smooth. Crush the garlic with the salt until a smooth paste is formed, and beat into the butter with the pepper.

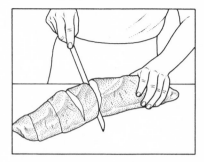

2 Partially cut through the loaf at 5 cm (2 inch) intervals. Liberally spread garlic butter in each incision.

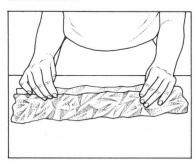

3 Wrap the whole loaf in foil and place in a warm oven for 15–20 minutes, until the butter has melted and flavoured the bread.

INDEX